By Waters of the South Fork

by

Daniel J. Stowe

Designed by M. C. Churchill-Nash

Laney-Smith, Inc., Publisher
Charlotte, North Carolina

Published by Laney-Smith, Inc.
1370 Briar Creek Road
Charlotte, North Carolina 28205

Phone: (704) 536-9832
Fax: (704) 536-9834

Distribution by: Daniel Jonathan Stowe Foundation, Inc.
          P. O. Box 1046
          Belmont, North Carolina 28012

          Phone: (704) 825-1437
          Fax: (704) 825-1578

Manufactured in the United States of America

Library of Congress Cataloging-in-Publication Data:

Stowe, Daniel J. (Daniel Jonathan), 1913-
     By Waters of the South Fork/by Daniel J. Stowe.
          p. cm.
     Includes bibliographical references and index.
     ISBN 1-891816-01-2
          1. Stowe, Daniel J. (Daniel Jonathan), 1913- 2. Stowe family. 3. Rhyne family. 4. Daniel
     Stowe Botanical Garden. 5. North Carolina—Biography. I. Title.

CT275.S8765 A3 2000
975.6'043'0922—dc21
[B]   00-062996

Credits:
     Design—M. C. Churchill-Nash
     Printing—Jostens Graphics, Charlotte, North Carolina
     Cover Photograph by Rick Haithcox Photography

Contents

Introduction

"**Textile magnate plans major botanical garden**" read the headline on the front page of *The Charlotte Observer*, Sunday, May 12, 1991. The facts of the story were that Daniel J. Stowe was setting aside 480 acres of rolling farmland on Lake Wylie, 18 miles southwest of uptown Charlotte, for a botanical garden "to rival the nation's finest." To bring even greater credence to his act, he had established the Daniel Jonathan Stowe Conservancy and donated a sufficient amount of money to begin construction of the project. This daring expression of philanthropy brought him into regional consciousness, and the development of the Daniel Stowe Botanical Garden has kept him there.

It was Wednesday, March 11, 1992 when I met Dan Stowe for the first time. Our meeting followed my initial letter to him and a sequence of phone conversations that began the preceding fall. The news stories heralding the botanical garden had spoken of his having two warehouses of historic memorabilia. Being a writer of history, I had read this with fascination and wanted to meet this exceptional preserver of the past. In the file at my office, my note summarizing that visit concluded with: "Renaissance man."

In this instance it is not a cliche, but an accurate description. I met a tall man of military bearing and a manner of marked courtesy. We conversed in his study at Seven Oaks Farm, some six miles from the town of Belmont and about two miles from the botanical garden. This room engrosses one with its rich wood paneling and architectural detailing. I was especially intrigued by a series of arched doors almost nine feet in height, each with magnificent carving. I gained some insight into this complex personality—a man born into wealth who had chosen to use money creatively. He was also the second son of a prominent father, Robert Lee Stowe Sr., a circumstance that is usually a challenge. The 1951 edition of *Who's Who of America* listed Stowe Sr. as president of three textile manufacturing companies and president of six additional corporations.

Even the Daniel Stowe Botanical Garden is an ambitious and artful way of being a steward of the land, his gift to today's and future generations.

This book of his memoirs is richly graphic, for Dan Stowe has been a collector all of his life. His home and warehouses store items such as his first train, his earliest camera, his family's first television set, to ancient architectural components, antique cars, books and furniture. Many of the illustrations are Dan's own photography, because he chose photography as a hobby when he was 17 or 18. Here you will read of his earliest memories from the age of two, his detailing of the two houses he shared with his parents, his days at Belmont Abbey College. His memories will bring to life the early days of Belmont, when families and friends congregated on front porches for fellowship. And you will read of the rebirth of the McAdenville Mill in 1939, bringing jobs to people still wounded by the Depression. The story of the gradual acquisition of land, the adventure into antiques known as "The Plantation House," the designing and building of the house at Seven Oaks Farm, donating carriages to the Dallas Museum—and finally the full story of the Daniel Stowe Botanical Garden—they are all told here in Dan Stowe's own words. Sometimes they occur as dialogues and at other times in his informal and anecdotal style. At the beginning of this adventure, Dan declared: "I can't write a book. But I can talk a book." He has—as dozens of audio tapes confirm.

Editor: Beth Laney Smith

Belk Stores Services Inc./2801 West Tyvola Road/Charlotte, N. C. 28217-4500/(704) 357-1000

Chairman of the Board

March 8, 1999

Ms. Beth Laney Smith
Chairman
Laney-Smith, Inc.
P. O. Box 18218
Charlotte, NC   28218

Dear Beth:

Dan is an enthusiastic leader. He has always thought about the growth
of the nation and its beauty. Not everyone thinks about beauty and the
future at the same time as Dan has done throughout his whole life.

It was a privilege for our father to have had a close friendship as well as
a business relationship with Dan's father. We have always been proud
of the success that the Stowe's have enjoyed and the many friends
and businesses they have acquired during their lifetime.

Dan will always be remembered for the beautiful garden and wonderful
inheritance he has continued for the world to enjoy.

What an honor and a privilege to have known a man of his stature.

Best wishes.

Sincerely,

John

John M. Belk

JMB/bc

These beginning pages, excerpts from interviews conducted by Lauren Brisby, present him through the eyes of friends and co-workers.

In the words of Robert Allison Ragan, longtime family friend and Gaston County Historian:

> *I just can't think of a nicer, more genuine person to talk about than Dan Stowe. I remember him being a very down-to-earth and approachable person, and this impressed me, as I was probably 25 years his junior. He was always "Dan" to me. I don't think I ever called him anything other than "Dan." His sister was always "Mrs. Pharr." His brother, Robert, was always "Mr. Stowe." But Dan was always "Dan."*
>
> *Dan shared his artistic interest and love of beauty with his sister, Mrs. Catherine Pharr, whose talents along those lines were exquisite and legendary. I can well remember Dan and my mother, Jocelyn Sikes Ragan, talking about gardening. It seemed that whenever they would see each other or get together, they would get around to that subject eventually. They might even send samples of their horticultural delights to each other for inspection and suggestions. They were always trying different little things.*

James "Jick" Garland, longtime family friend and garden board member, elaborates on Dan's modesty:

> *He was reserved, but he was quite a social animal! We used to kid him about his "running around" car. He'd have these big, fine limousines, but when he went out for a date, he'd ride in a more modest car. He's never one to try to overimpress somebody!*
>
> *He is always a gracious host, and he and Alene have very elaborate parties. He likes fine foods and fine beverages. He is particularly interested in southern history, which is probably what allows him to expect and enjoy good food and service.*

Mrs. Ilena Pratt, executive secretary to the Stowe and Pharr family for 50 years, remembers her experiences working with Dan:

Dan has the best memory of anyone you will ever find. He is very thorough in everything. If he wanted to buy a new anything—a tractor, or build a new silo—he'd want to know the price of the old one, if it was 30 years ago. And he'd want me to bring him the figures. I'd say, "Well, you just tell me when." He'd tell me exactly the year and the month, and of course it was no trouble to find it then. He already knew the price to the dollar! He could remember everything!

As Johnnie Lowery, employee of the Bank of Belmont, founded by Robert Lee Stowe Sr., recalls:

He was very close to Hazel Stowe, George Stowe's second wife, who he referred to as Madame Butterfly. And she would refer to Dan as The Dreamboat!

I remember I had recently purchased a classic sports car. I called Alene to ask if she would like to go for a ride. Well, Dan had just purchased a Rolls Royce. He said that he would rather Alene not ride in the sports car, but that he would be happy to take us both out in his new Rolls. He didn't want his wife to be in a sports car! But that was fine with me because I got to ride in a new Rolls Royce.

I consider it a rare privilege to know Dan, and I consider him one of my best friends. He has an elegant humility, which I think is a real virtue. The world needs more Dan Stowes.

J.B. Holcomb, friend and personal employee, tells of his first impression of Dan:

After meeting Dan at a Christmas party at the McAdenville mill in the early 70s, I heard that he was in need of a caretaker for Seven Oaks. I went over to Dan's house and met with him concerning the position available. Dan was one of the finest country gentlemen I'd ever met. He was courteous. He was awfully nice to his employees. I never heard him raise his voice to any of them or to me. He thinks about your convenience. He's that way with all of his employees.

"I've decided I'm going to come out of retirement and take a job so I won't have to work so hard!"

— Dan Stowe

This quote provides insight into Dan's ever-present sense of humor. And words of friends and employees reveal both this trait and his vast kindness.

Vicki Funderberk, who has worked at Seven Oaks for about 10 years, tells of Dan's perpetual sense of humor:

*One night I made him a baked potato for dinner. He wasn't very hungry and he just didn't want to eat it. He sat there and made a little face on his baked potato with fixings and carvings. Then he called me out there and asked what I did to his potato before I served it to him. I looked at it, and it had this face on it. I said, "I did **not** do that! It did **not** look like that when I gave it to you!" He had a very straight face. I really almost panicked until he started laughing. He has a wonderful sense of humor.*

Sondra Schronce, an employee at Seven Oaks for over 12 years, tells of Dan's country-style diet, which among other things, includes pig's feet and sardines:

His favorite dish is "stinky" shad (laughs). You bake it about five hours and it stinks up the whole house! The first time I made it, I cleaned the whole kitchen because I thought something was bad wrong in there. Then I found out it was the fish. I was just about in tears because I was going to have to tell Mrs. Stowe the fish had gone bad and he couldn't have it for lunch. Then she told me it was supposed to

1998 Outstanding Philanthropist by the Charlotte chapter of the National Society of Fund Raising Executives. This honor was awarded to Dan for numerous philanthropic contributions to:

- Daniel Stowe Botanical Garden (1990)
- Arts & Science Council of Charlotte intended for use in the Blumenthal Performing Arts campaign (1991)
- Presbyterian Hospital Foundation (1993)
- Arts & Science Council (1994)
- Visitor Pavilion at the botanical garden (1997)
- YMCA East Gaston Branch (1998)
- Received theGertrude S. Carraway award by Preservation North Carolina (1998)

smell like that. Ugh! That is his favorite dish. He always calls Shirley Rankin, his secretary, to come and help him finish the shad. Those two, and Mr. Rankin, are the only ones who will eat it!

Robert Moss, a family friend and superintendent of housing at Stowe Pharr Mills, talks of building a wall for Dan on the river and the comfort he feels in Dan's presence:

He loves to talk about the old days. He likes to talk about the way they did things back then.

I went to Blair, South Carolina. I got him these big tongs. They were used by a blacksmith—my daddy was a blacksmith. It was the kind they make with an anvil—you could reach right into the fire and pick out a piece of red-hot coal with those things. He was tickled to death over those tongs!

I'm still good friends with him. I'll go there and walk right into his house. I can hardly stay away from him!

Shirley Rankin has been Dan's secretary and friend for more than a decade. Dan has come to depend on her for business transactions and personal support and guidance—not to mention making sure his socks are pulled up before taking a picture, which is how Shirley met Dan for the first time, while her husband Steve took his picture.

Before I went to work for Mr. Stowe, it was the 50th Anniversary of Stowe Mills Pharr Yarns, and they set up huge screens and flashed slides of employee photographs. I will never forget when they flashed the picture of Mr. Stowe in his navy uniform—it was like you could hear a pin drop. All these women gasped! It was dark, but you could hear that gasp of women because he was such a handsome man. I like to kid him about it now—all the women still swooning over him as a good-looking naval officer.

I've told him a lot of times, it's not like I am working for him, because I have so much fun. When I drive in that driveway, it's like I am in a different world—the serenity of going down that drive all the way up to the house. I feel like he trusts me, which makes me want to do everything possible within my knowledge and my ability to make sure it is done right.

Steve Rankin has been a friend and confidant to Dan, who also shares his interest of photography and film production.

We went up to Beach Mountain and spent three or four days up there. Before we went, he was telling Shirley, "You know, it will be cool up there. Take a sweater, because when the sun goes behind the mountain, it gets cool." And I told Shirley, "I just can't believe it is ever going to be cool." I am hot-natured, so I didn't take Mr. Stowe's word for it. I put an old window fan in the back of the van thinking, "I am going to stay cool!" (laughs) The window fan never came out of the van! We met him in the middle of the week at his mountain house and he saw the fan in the back of the van—he's kidded me about it ever since. He'll ask Shirley, "Going to the mountains this weekend?" After she tells him we are, he'll say, "Steve going to take the fan?"

He is the most kind and gentle person in the world. I am just fortunate to call him my friend.

Virgil Woods, property manager, his wife, Jane Woods, and Darrell Woods, their nephew, all work on the grounds of Seven Oaks. Each have been touched by the generous and kind spirit of Dan. Dan has built Virgil and Jane the log cabin they have dreamed of, and kept Darrell laughing as he chauffeurs him through downtown Belmont. Jane tells of Dan's fun and mischief:

Virgil has always dreamed of a log cabin. You probably noticed a log cabin on your way up here. Well, that's what he had always wanted. So Mr. Stowe found out about it. He built Virgil that log cabin. It is beautiful inside and outside. He does treat his employees like they are family. He always thanks you—whatever you do for him, he always thanks you.

The story Mr. Stowe always tells about how Virgil came to work at Seven Oaks is "God sent him." He prayed about it and believes God sent Virgil.

Not very many people have the combination that he has—a sense of humor, good-nature, cares about people, common sense—he's real smart.

God speaks to all individuals through what happens to them moment by moment.

—Jean Pierre de Caussade

History is merely a list of surprises. . . It can only prepare us to be surprised yet again.

—Kurt Vonnegut, Jr.

Memory can gleam, but never renew.—It brings us joys faint as in the perfume of the flowers, faded and dried, of the summer that is gone.

—H. W. Beecher

Someone said that God gave us memory so that we might have roses in December.

—J. M. Barrie

The greatest thing a human being ever does is to see something and tell what he sees in a plain way.

—John Ruskin

I've a grand memory for forgetting.

—Robert Louis Stevenson

We must always have old memories and young hopes.

—Arséne Houssaye

Chapter 1

At the Starting Line

**...there is properly no history,
only biography.**

—Ralph Waldo Emerson

In 1924, Mrs. Nellie Stowe purchased an expensive short suit for Dan. He explains, "It might not have cost more than $50, but that was expensive back then!" In fact, his mother was so proud of her purchase, she had him sit for this portrait in his new clothes. However, after Dan wore it to church on Sunday, Mrs. Stowe could never get him to wear it again. Dan remembers, "I've never been kidded so much in my life!" The suit was worn twice—once to the sitting of this portrait, and once to church.

The true history of a place lies in its people – in the challenges they faced, the successes they achieved, and the difficulties they endured. In this sense, Daniel Stowe could be considered a living history of Gaston County. His memories lend both depth and detail to an examination of the area's ascent through the twentieth century, and his accomplishments have helped to shape its path into the future. Few people can speak of the people and events of a place with more authority, and Dan's fondness for his subjects offers the reader a bridge between the rigidity of history and the passion and sincerity of the people who were, and continue to be, a part of that history.

Born in 1913, Daniel Stowe has seen firsthand how the major events of the past century have shaped Belmont and the rest of North Carolina's Piedmont region. His unique perspective celebrates the changes that have occurred over the last 100 years—examining the influences of events and technologies on the people and the culture of the area. Dan graciously offers the reader a chance to relive the events that shaped Gaston County,

MAIN STREET — BUSINESS SECTION.   BELMONT, N. C.

in everything from the introduction of the first air conditioner to the celebrations that marked the end of the Second World War. Daniel Stowe's memoirs are an opportunity to share not just in the past of Gaston County, but also in the ongoing story of the South.

I like to think in decades. Do you know that I've lived in every decade but one in this century? I was born in 1913. Now the decade from 1910 to 1920 was dominated by the First World War. Then the second decade was that of the 'roaring twenties.' Of course I wasn't involved in the roaring part of it, but I could see people flying around doing all these things – dancing, things like that.

While Dan often speaks of his youth with a certain air of nostalgia, he is certainly not a man who chooses to live in the past. He has an entire room at his Seven Oaks estate devoted to the newest tools of the information age, complete with a broad array of audio and video equipment and a giant video screen that descends from the ceiling at the touch of a button. He speaks of transferring old film clips to digital images with less trepidation than most people have for programming their VCR. Perhaps his confidence in dealing with the advances of technology is due in some way to his familiarity with it. He has been a part of the information age since its earliest sparks in 1920, when the first American radio broadcast out of station KDKA in Pittsburgh changed rural life forever.

In 1900, the first carload of automobiles arrived in Charlotte. As seen here, this exciting innovation affected downtown Belmont as well.

A hotel and dress shop, as seen here, graced the street of early downtown Belmont, along with Stowe Mercantile.

Dan's brother and sisters: Robert Lee Jr., Catherine, Lillian.

To me, the 1920's was the decade of radio. My cousin, Rhyne Little, lived right outside of Lincolnton in a place called Southside, and he ordered a complete set of parts. In those days, you'd buy a kit and make your own radio—so he did. He had to use headphones, of course, an outside aerial—things like that…I heard that first broadcast on KDKA, in November 1920…I was seven at the time, but I remember it well… Harding spoke on radio in the caucus that preceded the election of 1921… From then on, people just went wild over trying to obtain some kind of little radio.

Dan remembers with fondness the effects of the introduction of radio on his youth and on the people of the time. He describes tuning in to local broadcasts from WBT in Charlotte at noontime to catch the weather report, and the "Watch the Buicks Travel" motto of the local sponsor. But his earliest recollections deal not with radios, but with cars…

I can remember when I was two years old. In about 1915, my father bought a Cadillac touring car—seven passengers—and he wanted to take us to Asheville. He took the whole family, including Emma Jane Ross,

Bert Davis, longtime family friend and chauffeur, photographed in the garden of the North Main St. house.

Dan's sister Lillian Rhyne Stowe (1900-1908), whom he never knew.

my nursemaid, and our chauffeur, whose name was Charles Samuel Albertus Davis. To us he was always 'Bert.' Well, with all my family and Emma Jane and Bert, we about filled up that car.

At the time of their trip, the Stowe family included Dan's parents, his 13-year-old brother Robert, and his sister Catherine, who was 11. Dan's oldest sister, Lillian, passed away in 1908—five years prior to his birth. Bert, the family chauffeur, worked for the Stowe family for over 40 years, and was a special friend to Dan, who remembers with fondness the wisdom and common sense of the man who Dan says "taught me a lot of things."

In those days, owning a car was as prestigious as it was exciting—especially in the South. The very first two automobiles to ever be shipped to a southern state arrived in Charlotte only 15 years earlier, and, at the time of their adventure, cars were far from being a common sight on the North Carolina landscape.

What I remember about going was the roads were very muddy. There were no paved roads, and a big rain came up. Well, we had to stop the car and put up the curtains. I think they were called isinglass curtains. You could see through the curtains—they kept the rain out. There was no heat in the car. Of course this was in June or July, so it was warm enough.

The Grove Park Inn in Asheville had been built in 1913, only two years before we made our trip. I was very impressed by the tremendous rock in there—the big rock fireplaces. I had never seen an elevator before, so naturally I wouldn't get in. Emma Jane had to carry me up and down the whole time we were there. I haven't liked elevators since.

But Dan's thoughts, like those of so many other American boys, quickly turned from a fascination with automobiles to a much more serious topic – war. At the start of World War I, Camp Greene was established in Charlotte – effectively doubling the city's population. The camp was located on the farm of James C. Dowd, whose home was used as the main headquarters. Between 1917 and 1919, as many as 60,000 troops could be found a Camp Greene at any given time, and Dan remembers well the impact this new city of soldiers had on the area.

The main road between Charlotte and Gastonia, Highway 7, came right by our house. The soldiers would march by our home on maneuvers. They had these great big trucks and they always had solid rubber tires on them. I never had seen that before, because most tires were pneumatic. They also had cannons and tanks going by there. It looked almost like a war zone. They had a lot of motorcycles with sidecars on them. I guess the sidecars were for the officers, for they had to follow along and they didn't want to be on the trucks. That's something you don't see today. I haven't seen one in years.

While most of us are well aware of the effects World War I had on the political and economic atmosphere of the day, it often takes a firsthand account to remind us how the war affected the lives of the people involved. Dan remembers both the fear of the war years and the jubilation felt at war's end.

The Stowe family lived in this house on Catawba St., equipped with one bathroom and an ornate base burner, capable of heating the entire house.

Robert Lee, Dan's father, with granddaughter Catherine Ann, at a festive occasion.

distractions during the first part of the century inspire images that Norman Rockwell might have portrayed. Recollections of the pleasures of growing up in Gaston County remind us that luxury can be as simple as a cold drink…

The iceman's name was George Hanks. I have some very pleasant memories of his visits. He would let all us kids in the neighborhood ride on the back of his ice wagon. We'd jump on and he didn't mind us doing it. It was a small adventure we all looked forward to.

There was no electric refrigeration then. We had a large, oak refrigerator that held 100 pounds of ice. It was delivered several times a week in an ice wagon drawn by a horse. The iceman didn't have to go into the house with it. We had an outside entrance up a pair of steps with a hole in the wall—he'd open that door, and it led directly into the refrigerator. He'd put that ice right through there. I've never seen that before or since. And under that ice were coils of pipe, through which water ran. We had a drinking fountain, and we had ice water all the time, which was very good for 1917.

All I heard was "Germany, Germany, Germany." Everybody was talking about it. And I thought that Germany was going to come over here. I didn't know there was an ocean between us, I guess. So I'd be afraid to go out in the yard. Bert said, "If any Germans come over here and you're out in the yard, I'll protect you." So any time Bert was in the yard, I'd go out there.

And then in 1918, when the war was over, the mills closed down to celebrate, and the people in the mill village got their big metal dishpans, like everyone had in those days, and were beating them like drums. They were walking down the road, in front of the houses, down Main Street, beating on dishpans. That made quite an impression on me.

The jubilation felt by all Americans at the end of World War I seemed to carry over through the 1920's, and while Dan admits he was not involved in the "roaring" part of the decade, his boyhood pastimes reflected the comfort and security of the time. Dan's memories of his boyhood

Even in those early years, it was clear that young Dan possessed the Stowe entrepreneurial spirit. When he wasn't busy riding on the ice wagon, Dan could be found tending his backyard flock or selling cold lemonade and coke to thirsty patrons at his front-yard refreshment stand on North Main Street in Belmont. His next door neighbor, George Howe, who was two years younger, gave him stiff competition with his own lemonade and coke stand. But by the end of the day, they would have merged their enterprises.

When I needed money, I'd ask my daddy and he'd let me have it. But I began making some of my own before I was 12. I set up a lemonade stand in front of our house on North Main Street and sold cokes as well as lemonade. Stowe Mercantile was just a few blocks away and I would go there and buy more when I sold out. I had my little store on wheels. I built it on an old wagon I had and could roll it around easily. I cleared about a dollar a day—that was a lot of money in those days!

I also raised chickens and things like that. I'd buy three or 400 baby chicks and they'd ship them to the post office. Before you could get to the post office, you'd hear the chickens. The post office people would say, "Are we glad to see you!"

Of course in that day everybody had chickens, and everybody had a cow. Nobody was delivering milk in those days. The Linebergers lived next door to us and they had a cow. Well, when the chickens grew up a bit, I'd sell them to people who came by and to stores. I kept my chicken business going until I was in high school.

I also raised homing pigeons, or squab, beginning this when I was twelve. I had a special pigeon feed that had a lot of peas in it. Little round peas. They lay two eggs every month, and they'd hatch 'em, and in four weeks they'd be able to fly away. My Dad loved the squab, so I'd supply him with them. There was a fellow in Charlotte who used to come out and buy them. He'd buy a dozen or so at a time from me.

Cornering the market on lemonade and squab was only a part-time pursuit, however. Most of Dan's days were filled with the social and academic demands of school. Due to some childhood health problems, he was educated under the private tutelage of a retired schoolteacher until the fifth grade. Entering into public school was quite a transition for Dan, who had grown accustomed to the quiet, one-on-one teaching he had received as a younger boy.

I had a lot of fights! In those days, boys did a lot of scrapping. I was a new fellow in the school, so they all wanted to try me out…I won some of them. And I lost some of them!

I really didn't begin to like school until I went to Belmont Abbey, and that was a delightful school. The most wonderful teachers—dedicated teachers. There was Father Benedict Rittger and Father Cuthbert Allen

As Dan recalls, Belmont Abbey was a very concentrated environment, with only four to five students for every teacher. Pictured here: At left, Father Leo Frierson; at right, Father Robert Brennan. (Photo from Belmont Abbey Archives.)

and Father Leo Frierson. I didn't know how to study until they taught me. And oh—Father Raphael Arthur. He was one of the finest professors I've ever seen breathe. Those people dedicate their life to that, you know. It was practically like having a private tutor. There might not be more than four or five in your class at a time.

Dan's boyhood was not all work and no play, however. Much the same as any boy of today, Dan could often be found skating, playing sports, and hanging-out with friends. When it comes to boys having fun, it seems that the passage of time becomes a little less meaningful.

I loved roller-skating and that's what I did every afternoon—roller-skating and bicycle riding. That's why my knees are bad now—roller-skating. I thought I was an expert at it—turning in circles. I also tried tap dancing and ballroom dancing, but was never good at either one. Tap dancing was the rage then, made popular by movie stars. We also played ball at school, and in the afternoons—baseball, football, basketball—whatever was in season.

The drugstore, that was our clubhouse. We'd go down there after school, and then after supper we'd go back down there. We'd all meet at the drug store—Robinson Drug Company and also Belmont Drug Company. Robinson was the one I think we went to more.

Dan was even known to get into a little mischief at times…

Now when I think back, I feel a little guilty about some pranks I played upon my sister and her boyfriends. She was dating two men pretty steadily, and when one of them would come, I'd set the other one's picture out in the room. And I wired the sofa. I would hide behind it and then when they were seated, I'd deliver a shock… It was just a light tingle, it didn't hurt.

Dan was also known to frequent the movie theatres as a young man. With the introduction of air conditioning in the late 1920's, seeing a picture became an even more enjoyable pastime…

Refrigerated air conditioning must have come out around 1928. My first experience with it was at the old Carolina Theatre, which was the first building in Charlotte to be air-conditioned. It was cold, like walking into a refrigerator, when we went over there one night to see some of the pictures that first came out. I think they were blowing air over ice, because it was humid. It was not dry air conditioning. They got that eliminated before long—that damp feeling—and you felt the fresh air conditioning that you feel today. I remember there was a show called "Lilac Times," and another one, "Wings." And Al Jolson sang "Mammy."

But the comfort and prosperity of the post war years would come to an abrupt end in 1929, when the stock market crashed and plunged the United States into the Great Depression. As the people of Gaston County suffered along with the rest of the country, Dan remembers how the Depression brought neighbors together to overcome the hardships they faced as a community. The mills played a central role in the local economy at the time, and Dan saw firsthand the importance of the mills to local families.

*And then of course in 1929 the Crash came. And the thirties was the decade of the depression. It was a **remarkable** decade because people became so dependent upon each other. Everybody had a garden and swapped vegetables, and they got by. There was a closeness there that I don't think we ever had after that.*

My father was in the mill business, but they couldn't sell their yarn. They'd spin it and keep piling it up in the mill until it reached the ceiling. But he ran it just enough so that people would have a little income and be able to get something to eat. And the people were appreciative of being able to get some income.

I know at McAdenville—we bought that company in 1939—those people had really been through it because that mill hadn't run in two or three years. Of course the county at that time gave them a little bit of supplement. Everybody that was really in need got a little check. When we got things started that was the happiest bunch of people—and the finest people.

Father Leo Frierson.

Dan remembers the professors of Belmont Abbey fondly. Left, Father Raphael Arthur; right, Father Francis Underwood.

Father Raphael Arthur.

Father Cuthbert Allen.

Father Benedict Rittger on the lawn of Belmont Abbey.

Above photos courtesy of Belmont Abbey Archives.

Even through the hardships of the Depression, the Stowes were able to find time for travel as a family. Through the twenties and thirties, Dan and his family enjoyed numerous trips outside the state, and it was on these trips that Dan first began to appreciate antiques and collectibles.

My family took train trips to New York City at least once a year. But I think my favorite trips were driving to Florida, where my daddy had a little orange grove. He liked to go down there in March, when the fruit was getting ripe… It was during these trips that I went with my mother to look

Dan's 1962 Thunderbird convertible.

over antiques. She really had a good eye. I would tease her by saying: "Now what do you want with that old worn-out furniture?" Within a few years, I was seeing pieces I wished I had the money to buy. This led me to search out architectural components, which appealed to me even more than furniture.

As with his trip to Asheville years before, Dan remembers the cars the family traveled in with fondness.

One of the cars my father was driving then was a seven passenger Lincoln, and I think it was as long as from here to the front door. They haven't made them since the thirties…

While Dan may like to think in decades, it quickly becomes apparent during conversation that he marks the passage of time by the automobile as well.

America's love affair with the car came about 1910, 1920, 1930—and it continues. I still like cars. One of my dad's early cars was made by Mr. E.M. Flanders, but everybody called it "EMF." Bert nicknamed the EMF the "Early Morning Failure" because he had to crank it. Cars didn't have self-starters.

My father bought a 1914 Ford with a brass radiator, and I hated to see him sell that car. I hope someday I'll be able to buy one—if I can find one. I have some old cars I've been saving. My mother's golden wedding anniversary present was a seven-passenger 1949 Cadillac, and I have it over there in the warehouse. I have an English taxi that's really old, that I got over in England. I have a 1962 Thunderbird Roadster—red—and it's still in good shape. And there are several more, including a '72 Cadillac.

I was 17 when I had my first car. It was a Ford Model A Coupe. I was graduated from high school that same month, so I got the car. Later I sold it and after some 30 years regretted that action. So now I have another one exactly like it, which I found in the mountains some years back. It's in my warehouse.

Nellie Rhyne Stowe, on her 50th wedding anniversary, with her new Cadillac. Dan remembers this as one of the "finest" automobiles his family ever owned.

Just as every decade has a car, every car has a story. One story in particular makes Dan laugh even today.

Do you remember when cars had a spark and a throttle on the steering wheel column? You could get more spark when you got ready to start it, you know. We had this fellow working for us—we'll call him Rufus. People told me he had more brawn than he had brain. My brother Robert had this brand-new 1933 Cadillac with this lever on top of the steering wheel where he could increase the spark. One day Rufus was out there and broke it off. So Robert, he just—oh, he thought it was

terrible. So he bought a new one and had it installed. And he came to Rufus and said, " I want you to come out and show me how you did that." So Rufus took the lever with a mighty twist and broke it off again! I'd give anything if I had a picture of Robert's face!

Dan's association with automobiles in the area reads like a history of cars in the South. The very first automobiles to arrive in any southern state were delivered to a Mr. Osmond L. Barringer of Charlotte in November of 1900. According to accounts presented in *The Hornet's Nest,* by LeGette Blythe and Charles R. Brockman, these two steam-driven Locomobiles were succeeded in 1902 by a pair of

Belmont Drug Co. and Robinson Drug Co., in the heart of downtown Belmont, were two popular gathering places for Dan as a teenager.

single-cylinder Oldsmobile roadsters. The Stowe family purchased their first automobile about ten years later, which made the Stowes one of the earliest families to have their own automobile in all of the South. Dan's thoughts of these first automobiles are deeply intertwined with his memories of the area.

Dan relied on his father and earlier generations to recount the days of horse and buggy. Pictured here is Laban Jonathan Rhyne. (Courtesy of Ermintrude Little Mullen.)

When my father and mother would drive to Charlotte, they used big lap robes. Of course before that were the horse and buggy days. My father said that when he was a boy, his family would start out to Charlotte in the middle of one day and go to their uncle's right across the river. They would spend the night with him, and then they'd go into town early the next morning.

The arrival of the automobile brought with it many changes to the Gaston County area. Dan remembers bits and pieces of the old horse and buggy days, mainly those passed on to him from his father. From sturgeons to whiskey making, it is clear that the Gaston County of Dan's parents and grandparents is a world away from the Gaston County of today.

When my daddy first went over to Charlotte, I think it was in a wagon, because my grandfather, C.T. Stowe, would take over certain supplies to sell and then he'd buy

things to bring back. One thing that amazed me was—once in a while he'd catch a sturgeon from the Catawba River, and that's unheard of now, you know. A sturgeon would weigh 100 pounds or more and would bring a big price in Charlotte. Since they put the dams in, sturgeon can't come up the river anymore.

My grandfather farmed. He had some help. There were no slaves on the Stowe side of the family. Now on his mother's side, the Sloans that lived over on Steele creek—they had some. But my grandfather just hired people to work for him. Then he bought a lot of land. At one time, he owned much of the land in Belmont. And at that time he would sell out parcels of it. My father said that if he had kept it a little bit longer, he would have made more. In those days you would probably sell land for as little as ten dollars an acre.

There was little industry here 'til after the Civil War. Do you know what the biggest industry was in this county? Making whiskey. Because there were so many streams coming into the county, you know, and that's where they'd grind up the meal and make the whiskey. I read somewhere that it was the biggest whiskey-producing county in North Carolina. And then textiles came in.

While Belmont grew rapidly through the early 1900s, it retained much from the quieter times of Dan's father and grandfather. But the tranquility of the small town of Belmont was shaken yet again in the 1940s with the onset of World War II. Dan was called away from the area for the longest period of his life, and like many of his fellows, saw his community, and even the world, change seemingly before his eyes.

World War II was a time to show your patriotism. The men and women of Gaston County were as heroic as their ancestors had been in other wars. The period of the forties was a time of displacement—men off to training and to war, often their wives relocated to be with their husbands as long as possible. I was away from Gaston County for the longest period of my life, serving as a naval officer assigned to Charleston and later to Washington.

And then the fifties was a great decade, because we were all out of that. People who were raised up during the Depression and the war years could relax and get their businesses in order. But it was also detrimental in a way because mothers and fathers would say:" I've been through two hard decades and I'm not going to let my children live like I did." So then they spoiled them in the fifties. This is my personal opinion. But each decade has had its own personality.

Despite the challenges it faced through the years, Belmont remained a close community, and the kind of place its citizens were proud to call home, Dan being no exception.

Belmont was a very small town, of course, a rural community. We lived just across the street from the First Presbyterian Church, where we were members. And that's where the social activity was. Back in those days, all our friends would get together at church, for a lot of different functions—picnics, things like that. It was a time when people were really closer to each other. You could walk up and down the street and people would be sitting on their front porches. They weren't in their cars going to Charlotte like they are now. It was a delight to be able to walk down the street and see all your friends on their front porches. It's an entirely different kind of life, and I think we've lost something.

The downtown section of Belmont is just about gone. In the old days, almost any afternoon, you couldn't find a parking space in Belmont. They had a great big place out there where all the farmers congregated, and they'd have a big time swapping stories. Belmont was the place to be in those days, which is why my father built the new house close to town.

Belmont was so much the place to be that I continued my education at Belmont Abbey College, as I said earlier. For two years, in addition to required courses, I took such subjects as anatomy and biology—anything related to medicine. At that time Belmont Abbey was a junior college, but I enjoyed that environment so much that I stayed on for a year after graduating from the two-year course.

It is this feeling of community and sense of place that has inspired in Daniel Stowe such a sense of stewardship for the Belmont area. Dan has spent his life promoting the economic and social development of the area, and knows as well as anyone the importance of keeping a community focused on the future without neglecting its past. Dan's love for the Belmont community and its people becomes particularly apparent in his descriptions of his former homes and neighborhoods. The Stowe homes are a true reflection of the area itself, maintaining a stately southern tradition while, at the same time, embracing new technologies and the social changes those technologies inspire.

Robert Lee Stowe in front of the North Main Street home.

I have memories of our Catawba Street home when I was about two. It was heated with a base burner located in the hallway, and you could look in it and see the coals. Beautiful thing. If the doors were left open, the base burner heated the whole house. I bought one just like it a few years back and took it to the mountain house. On Catawba Street we had one bathroom, put in about 1901 when the Chronicle Mill was built. Water was run from the mill. This house is still in good condition.

In 1916 my father hired an architect to design a new house for us. He was J.M. McMicheal, who had his office in Charlotte. He had designed our church, First Presbyterian of Belmont, which was built in 1913. Our house was finished in 1917, when I was about four. I can remember moving to the new house. I didn't like it. I wanted to go back to the old one. But this was a much bigger house and I soon discovered that it had some special innovations that appealed to me.

It was a large, Georgian-style brick residence with fluted columns on the front terrace and also in the porte-cochere. It originally had a slate roof but was recently changed to copper. The house was built on a beautiful lot, 200 feet long, fronting on Main Street, and it went back about 400 feet on Woodrow Street. It was decorated and furnished by Parker-Gardner of Charlotte, an old concern over there. They did decorating and sold nice furniture and things.

The grounds were landscaped by an English landscape architect who lived in Charlotte. His name was Mr. Lee Colyer. He built several hundred feet of pergolas, and brick walls within these pergolas. They all had Tuscan columns. And then in addition to the pergolas, we had something called a summerhouse. It was up at a higher level. When you went down a pair of steps into the main garden, you could see a fountain in the distance. The summerhouse had half-fluted columns and a rotunda on the top. All of that's gone now. Within the last 30 or so years, after my mother and father became ill, termites or something got in there and wrecked it.

The beauty of the Stowe homes is easily apparent from Dan's vivid descriptions, but they are equally striking for their conveniences and unique details. Dan's residences have always included a variety of practical designs and gadgetry, in addition to meticulous architectural detail. Dan has studied and collected architectural components for many years, and has developed quite an eye for architectural detail.

Of course in those early days, there was no air conditioning. But we had big windows and high ceilings and cross ventilation. There have been lots of changes, but I guess every generation has something to offer. It's much easier to live now. My father said he had lived through the time when you had to throw a pine knot on the fire to read by, when he was a boy, and he liked it better now—because of air conditioning and things like that. I think electricity is one of the greatest things that ever happened.

Another thing that was sort of new at that time: the kitchen door had an electric lock on it. When the cook would come, early in the morning, she would ring the buzzer that would sound in my daddy's room. He'd press a button and the door would fly open, without his having to go downstairs to let her in.

There was a laundry chute on the top floor, where the bedrooms were, which allowed clothes and linen to drop to the basement.

The architectural details of the new house didn't mean much to me when I was four. Later I came to admire the large entrance hall with its view of a somewhat dramatic stairway. Its first section came to a landing with a large sunburst window. Then the stair branched to either side, giving double access to the hallway upstairs, off which were the bedrooms. I very soon realized that I had many more possibilities for play in all the spaces of this new house.

Editor:
David M. Munson

The North Main Street house is now the home of Robert Lee Stowe, Dan's nephew.

Chapter 2

Hearth and Home

As newlyweds, Mr. and Mrs. R. L. Stowe honeymooned at Niagara Falls in 1899.

"A happy family is but an earlier heaven," wrote Bowring[1]—and I feel as if he must have known mine. Looking back on my life after 86 years, the areas that warm my heart invariably center around my family. My first memories are of life with Papa, Mother, Robert, and Catherine, in our home on 135 North Main Street, and these remembrances are very special to me. Even after I grew up, the family remained my anchor—the group in which I could always be myself, whether enjoying a good belly laugh or airing my grievances. They were always there for me.

---

[1] English Statesman, Sir John Bowring (1792-1872)

Bill Pharr, Dan's brother-in-law;
Robert L. Stowe III and Harding, sons
of Dan's only brother; and brother
Robert L. Stowe, Jr.

Catherine Stowe Pharr, on her wedding day.

As my brother and sister started families of their own, our traditions evolved, but the heart of our activity always revolved around my parents' house. On Sundays, after attending church services, all of us gathered at 135 North Main Street for lunch. My sister Catherine and her husband, Bill Pharr, came to these meals, along with their two children, Catherine Ann and Bill Pharr, Jr. My brother, Robert, and his wife, Ruth, always had their three boys in tow—Robert Lee III, Harding, and Richmond. In later years, Catherine Ann brought her husband, Bip Carstarphen, and their three children: Martin, young Catherine, and Bill. We filled that dining room!

Family sometimes even played a role in my social life; my cousins Ted and Bill Stowe and I would take our dates out together. My relatives would probably be glad to share some amusing stories from those days, but this is only a memoir—not a confession!

While exploring the terrain of genealogy is not the objective of this book, some commentary about the Stowes and the Rhynes who came before me will provide insight into the fabric of my life.

Two Stowe Brothers Enter North Carolina About 1800

The Stowe family came here from Virginia about 1800. Two brothers, Abraham and Jacob Stowe (sons of William Stowe II), both settled near the west bank of the South Fork River, not far from the South Carolina line. In Virginia, they left behind two brothers and two sisters—which is just as well, because Abraham and Jacob alone populated Gaston history with descendants named Stowe.

Dan and his sister-in-law, Ruth Stowe, in the
library of his Seven Oaks house.

While walking though Stowesville Cemetery, visitors may take notice of the Stowe family lineage dating back to the 1700s.

two or more wives being recorded for some of my ancestors. But in spite of these trials, the families did multiply. I counted 55 members of the Stowe family listed in the 1998 Belmont phone directory.

Colonel Jasper Stowe

One of Larkin's sons was Colonel Jasper Stowe, born February 27, 1821. My aunt, Minnie Stowe Puett, described Jasper in her book, *History of Gaston County*:

> *Jasper Stowe was a plain unassuming man, free from vanity, full of simplicity, and eager to be of service. Governor Vance said to him during the war [the War Between the States]: 'Stowe, you shall not go to the army. No man in the South can take your place where you are.'*

Jasper was also important in the early history of textiles in Gaston County. He was the first person from what is now Gaston to build a mill and enter the cotton manufacturing business. However, the mill that he built on the South Fork River in 1847 or 1848 was in adjoining Lincoln County. When that mill was closed and its machinery moved, about 1853, to the Stowe lands along the South Fork River in Gaston County, it represented the third cotton mill in Gaston. It had been preceded by Mountain Island Mill (ca. 1848) and Woodlawn Factory (ca. 1852).[2] Stowe's Factory, as it was called, changed ownership several times before its site was covered over by backwaters from the Duke Power dam.

Descendants of Abraham Stowe

My own branch of the family descended from Abraham Sr. (1762-1841), Jacob's brother. Abraham married three times. His second wife, Lettie Tucker of Virginia, bore him eight children. One of their sons was Jacob Reece Stowe, who was born in Nottoway County, Virginia, in 1809. Of the eight children by Jacob Reece's first wife, Sarah Marriner Stowe, one was my grandfather, Charles Theodore Stowe (1833-1907), known as "Dory."

Dory served in the Civil War, and after it ended in 1865, he married Margaret Ann Sloan of Mecklenburg County. Eight of their 13 children lived to adulthood: Robert Lee Sr. (April 5, 1866-March 9, 1963), Samuel Pinckney, Minnie Stowe Puett, Ida Octavia, Mary Emma, James William, Susan Ada, and George W. All four brothers got their start in business with the Stowe Mercantile Company in Belmont. Thereafter, they all played major roles in the textile industry, following the example of my father.

Descendants of Jacob Stowe

Larkin Stowe

Jacob had nine children, one of the most notable being Larkin, who was born on August 20, 1788. Larkin represented Lincoln County in the House of Commons in 1842, and in the Senate in 1844 and 1846. During that time, he introduced the bill to separate Gaston County from Lincoln. In 1854, he served as Councilor of State.

Larkin had 15 children by two different wives. While this number of children now seems large, it was the way they did things in those days. Also, many people died in childhood at that time. When you visit old cemeteries, it is distressing to see the lineup of tiny graves in the family plot. Men generally outlived women back then, due to fatal complications that sometimes arose during childbirth. This resulted in

[2] Robert Ragan, Gaston County Historian

Charles Theodore "Dory" Stowe, Dan's grandfather, served in the Civil War.

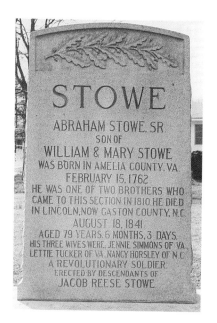

Dan's branch of the family stems from Abraham Stowe Sr., his great-great-grandfather.

My grandfather's place was about two miles southeast of Belmont. He built a new house and moved in during August 1880, living there until his death in 1907. This is known as "the Stowe place," and it was here that practically all the family was reared. The house today is designated by a historic marker.

In that day, men took great pride in their marksmanship. One of the best shots of all was Dory Stowe, who on a country stroll once brought down 12 distant squirrels with 12 shots of his rifle.[3]

The plaque in front of what is known as "the Stowe place," which still stands near Belmont and is considered a historical landmark.

---

[3] Cope and Wellman: p. 78.

Dan's father with his three brothers and one sister, from left to right: Jim Stowe, Robert Lee Stowe, Sue Stowe, Pinckney Stowe, George Stowe.

Robert Lee Stowe, Sr.

My father wrote of his life and times in *Early History of Belmont and Gaston County, North Carolina.* Following his death, *Robert Lee Stowe: Pioneer in Textiles* was written by LeGette Blythe, describing my father's career, and his civic and church leadership. His numerous and diverse achievements are well-documented there. Samuel Pinckney Stowe, his brother, and Abel Caleb Lineberger shared in the leadership of launching textile mills. At one time they operated 20 mills, which was the largest chain in the county.

The R. L. Stowe Bridge, located on the South Fork River, was built in 1948. It bears a plaque that reads: "...in recognition of long and outstanding service to Gaston County." That service included his position on the Board of County Commissioners beginning in 1914—a position that he held for 41 years. He was its chairman from 1922 until his 89th birthday, in 1955. He served on the Belmont school committee longer than anyone could remember, and was a deacon of the First Presbyterian Church and its treasurer from the mid-1890s until his death. Yet in all his life, my father never moved more than three miles from the house in which he was born.

In spite of these heavy commitments, Papa always had time for me. I learned much about plants and animals from him, because he always considered himself, by first calling, a farmer. He encouraged all the small business ventures I undertook, including the raising of chickens and pigeons. And of course, I could not have acquired my acreage without his endorsements of loans.

Throughout his life, he would set aside all other distractions to listen to my latest problem and guide me toward resolution.

Where Stowes and Rhynes Came Together: Family Gatherings in My Parents' Home

The home of my parents was a magnet for family gatherings. Firelight and the savory aromas of cooking food created a welcoming atmosphere. William James "Bill" Pharr, Jr., and Catherine Ann, the children of my sister, were the first grandchildren in the family. She recently shared her memories of "the good times."

Catherine Ann Carstarphen:

We've always had a close family. When I was a little girl, every Sunday we had dinner at my grandmother's house. Everybody had his or her specialty. My grandmother made chicken salad, and Dan and my father competed with each other on baked beans. We had fun in the kitchen.

There were just two children then—my brother and me. Dan and my other uncle, Robert Stowe, waited a long time to get married, so they both were bachelors. That was back when there was no television—and certainly no VCR. The times were different. But there was always a lot going on down there for a little girl and her brother!

Dan and his niece, Catherine Ann, with her father, Bill Pharr.

Catherine Ann Carstarphen, Dan's niece, daughter of his sister.

At that time in the school system, if you lived close enough, you could walk home to lunch, so we always walked to my grandmama's for lunch and then walked back.

Christmastime was especially exciting. Robert and Dan usually had dates, and we would go down and help them decorate the Christmas tree every year. That was fun for us as children. Robert always put a train under the tree—that was the last thing we did.

On Christmas Day, we would go back for dinner, and there would be a fire going in the fireplace. My brother and I sat at a card table for many years, until we were old enough to graduate to the big table. In fact, I can remember wanting to go to the big table. And then when I got there, I had to wait so long for the food to be served that I thought, "Why did I want to do this?" I learned a lot of manners there!

My grandmother was a wonderful entertainer, and she loved beautiful things. The china and crystal would be laid out, and all of the food would be served, and it

Catherine Pharr with her daughter, Catherine Ann, and son, Billy, at the North Main Street home.

Catherine Ann Carstarphen with husband, J. M. "Bip" Carstarphen.

was just beautiful. Grandmama had a grape-fruit and avocado salad that she would serve at Christmas. And we always ate ambrosia—with the coconut—for dessert. That was good. She also had fruitcake, which I'm sure was homemade. There were two kinds—a white fruitcake and a dark fruitcake—and both were good. They cooked those fruitcakes early and let them season. A lot of people don't like fruitcake, but I love it—and I guess that's because I remember eating it as a child. And rolls—I remember wonderful yeast rolls. We always ate a big lunch!

These were happy times that I spent with my family. In some ways it doesn't seem so long ago.

Even after Bip and I were married and had our own children, we ate Sunday dinner at my grandparents' house. We never had too much of the hospitality they expressed.

Catherine Stowe Pharr Carstarphen, Catherine Ann's daughter.

Children of the family longed to enjoy the elegance in the living room arranged for holiday festivities.

Harding is the second son of my brother, Robert. Today he is president and chief executive officer of R. L. Stowe Mills, Inc. He also journeyed into the past to share his memories.

Harding Stowe:

I was born in 1956, and we lived in the same area where Dan lived. Our house was not actually on any street. It was centered on a piece of property with a little pond in back of my grandparents' home. My father had built it as a guest house for business visitors, whether they came from New York, Philadelphia, or Charlotte. After he got married, he moved into it, and it became a family house rather than a guest house. My mother still lives there.

Though Dan had an apartment in Charlotte and a place at the river, his primary residence was with his parents at 135 North Main Street.

As far back as I can remember, my grandparents required medical help. A staff of people was always there, because both my grandfather and grandmother had a stroke. Mrs. Lee was in charge of both medical and non-medical personnel. She was a very nice person, and we kidded around with her and the rest of the staff. Lena Forney was the cook—a real southern, country cook. She prepared things like good fried chicken, rice and gravy, and all these vegetables. I would love to have a meal like that today. At that time, I preferred to eat junk food. Dan used to kid me about it all the time, saying he would pay me a nickel for every green bean I would eat.

There were three of us kids who played together: my older brother, Robert; Martin Carstarphen; and myself. Martin is Catherine Ann's oldest son and is my age. Usually for lunch or dinner, we ate at a different table from our parents. If they ate in the formal dining room, then we ate in the informal dining room. If they were in the informal dining room, we usually ate in the kitchen. My

Harding Stowe, Dan's nephew.

grandparents were wonderful people even though they had some medical problems at that time. My parents were there, Catherine Ann and Bip, Mr. and Mrs. Pharr, Dan—it was a very nice family event.

Martin, Robert, and I used to love taking off and getting out from under the adults' view. We would explore the house, explore the garage. There was an apartment attached to that house. It's no longer there. My father and Dan, when they were both living there as bachelors, didn't want to entertain in the main house. So they built the apartment, and it was really nice. It had one great big room, with stereo and television. The property around the house was also fun to explore. At that point, it began to be kind of "let go," and some of it was covered with vines.

After my grandparents passed away, all of the families went in different directions. We continued to have Thanksgiving and holiday meals together, and some birthdays or special occasions, but it was no longer a weekly type of thing where the whole family was together.

Martin Carstarphen, oldest son of Catherine Ann.

Dan Explores the Rhyne Family

My mother's father was Laban Jonathan Rhyne, born in 1849—and I actually have movies of him talking. (Yes, you are reading correctly.) We bought a sound camera in 1937, and he was still alive then. I wish I'd asked him different questions and tried to find out more about what he remembered of the Civil War. He was about 12 when the war broke out—too young to go into the army. His job was to hide the silverware and the horses and such, as the Yankees came through.

The Rhyne (or Rein) family is of German origin. Grandfather Laban married Margaret Hoffman, who was also of German descent. Laban was a land owner and farmer living near Laboratory in Lincoln County. He had four children. The first was my mother, Nellie Lee Rhyne Stowe, who lived from April 11, 1876 to October 20, 1964. She was followed by Paul Conrad, Selena Pearl, and Florence Ermintrude.

Dan's niece and nephew, Catherine Ann and Billy. (Courtesy of Catherine Ann Carstarphen.)

Dan's Aunt Florence Rhyne, at age 18, in 1905.

Visits with Great-Aunt Florence and Great-Grandfather Rhyne

In his later years, Laban Rhyne lived with his daughter Florence in Lincolnton, and it was there that family gatherings took place. Catherine Ann was a small child then but remembers these happy times well:

Aunt Florence was a warm, gracious, wonderful hostess. She was both artistic— she could paint—and musical. We always looked forward to going to Lincolnton, because to a little girl it seemed a long way. (And I'm sure it was back then, because that was before they built many of the roads that we have today.) It was always cold at Christmastime, and we would be very excited about going to her house. My brother and I were the only little children in the family then. Aunt Florence had a daughter whose name was Ermintrude, and I think she's maybe ten

Laban Jonathan Rhyne opens a gift with the help of Catherine Ann as family members watch, from left to right: (seated) M. L. Little, husband to Aunt Florence; Laban Jonathan Rhyne, grandfather to Dan; Catherine Ann Pharr, daughter of Catherine Stowe Pharr; "Billy" Pharr, brother to Catherine Ann; (standing) Catherine Pharr, sister to Dan; Lena Little, aunt to Dan; Dan Stowe; Robert Little, cousin to Dan.

or 15 years older than me. But Bill and I were the little children, so we got a lot of attention from the adults.

When Aunt Florence opened the front door, we were always met by the wonderful smell of good food. And oh! she was so glad to see you. She was fluttering around making everybody happy. She would have a Christmas tree, and I remember singing carols. In her dining room, she would have food laid out, but we would always have to wait before eating. Her husband, M. L. Little, loved to ask the blessing. And he would ask a beautiful blessing, but it would be long. We would be thinking, "Golly, when can we eat?" I can remember that as such a warm experience, in spite of the wait.

I also loved to go there in the summertime. Aunt Florence's house had a long back porch, where she would serve lemonade. She had chickens and animals in the yard, as well as kittens. Playing there was always fun.

Jacob Rhyne First in this Area

Going back even further, the first Rhyne in this area was Jacob, who settled on upper Hoyle's Creek about 1794. He fathered eight children, and his son Jacob Jr. had nine.

When asked about my lineage, I simply say I'm a descendant of Moses Rhyne, who was born in 1812 and lived in Mt. Holly. He was my great-grandfather, and that seems far enough back to trace. Moses was one of 10 children born to Jacob Rhyne III. And he in turn did his share to populate the county, having seven children by his first wife, Margaret Hoffman, and four by his second wife, Mary Springs. He was one of six partners in Gaston County's second cotton factory, the Woodlawn, in 1852. So both sides of my family pioneered the local textile industry.

Daniel E. Rhyne

One of the most notable and colorful members of the Rhyne family in recent years was Daniel E. Rhyne, who was my grandfather Laban's brother. He was born in 1852 in a bedroom of the family farmhouse. His father, Moses, and Frederick Hoffman owned the Hoffman-Rhyne mercantile store at Mt. Holly. It was there that a meeting was held in 1842 to consider the question of dividing Lincoln County. Out of this meeting grew the political action that in 1846 resulted in the creation of Gaston County from the southern portion of Lincoln County.

From the June 1923 issue of Lincolnton's General Hardware Store News:

Mr. D. E. Rhyne Owns First Auto in State

The Lincoln Journal of November, 1899, published the following:

Mr. Dan E. Rhyne received his automobile Friday and has since been diligently at work, assisted by Mr. A. M. Price, in taming it. As soon as they get it trained to keep in the middle of the road and break it from climbing trees, Mr. Rhyne is going to take a ride. The possession of the first and only automobile in the State is adding considerably to Mr. Rhyne's popularity—all want to take a ride.

Mr. Rhyne is not only first in automobile ownership in the State but is first in many ways. He is a pioneer in the cotton mill business and his success has been wonderful. A financial genius, his keen judgment and foresight has enabled him to go forward and take advantage of low markets when others held back.

Mr. Rhyne is not only noted for his great financial strength but equally as much for his gifts to churches and colleges. His recent gifts to Lenoir-Rhyne College will make it an A grade institution.

If the board should decide to move the college from Hickory, Lincoln county would count it one of the greatest events in her history if the school was located here.

In recognition of his contributions, Lenoir-Rhyne College has dedicated the Daniel Efird Rhyne Memorial Building to Dan's namesake. (Courtesy of Lenoir-Rhyne College.)

Daniel Rhyne (1852-1933), was a successful textile and mining businessman and benefactor to what is now Lenoir-Rhyne College. (Courtesy of Ermintrude Little Mullen.)

In spite of the hardships of the War Between the States and the ensuing Reconstruction, Dan Rhyne attended the North Carolina College, a Lutheran-sponsored school at Mt. Pleasant, in 1872. By 1875 he was associated with his older brother, Abel P. Rhyne, in the construction of the Mount Holly Cotton Mill. It succeeded, and in 1883 they erected the Tuckaseege Mill. But shortly afterward, Dan sold his interest and turned his business attentions to Lincoln County. By the 1880s, Lincolnton was in a decline, losing its earlier vibrancy to Charlotte. Daniel Rhyne moved to Lincoln County in 1885 to build Laboratory Cotton Mill, which in a few years employed 125 people. Two additional mills followed: the Lincoln Cotton Mill, called "Southside," and the Daniel Manufacturing Co. The three mills gave jobs to 400 people and greatly boosted the economy.

Although his textile holdings in Lincoln and Gaston Counties grew extensively, Daniel Rhyne had other busi-ness interests as well. He owned and operated a tin mine just two miles south of Lincolnton, which was the only tin mine in North America. In 1916 he became the owner of the Piedmont Wagon Works in Hickory, which became one of the largest vehicle-manufacturing companies in the South. He owned a mica mining company in Mitchell County. In the textile scene, he owned or had financial interest in 24 manufacturing companies.

All of this success led to his becoming a benefactor of Lenoir-Rhyne College, originally known as Lenoir College. Beginning in 1904 and continuing through the 1920s, Dan Rhyne made such significant financial contributions to the school that he distinguished himself as its chief patron. The institution's name was officially changed to Lenoir-Rhyne College, in his honor, in August 1924.

When Dan Rhyne died in 1933, he left a multi-million dollar estate.

Dan and Alene pictured in 1998 at their annual family Christmas party.

The Story of Dan and Alene

When meeting with the editor on October 22, 1999, Dan and his wife, Alene (b. Mary Alene Nobles on November 18, 1938), looked back on the way they met and the love they have shared over the years since.

Dan: Alene and I were introduced to one another by a mutual friend at Myrtle Beach, and we went out to dinner that night.

Alene: That was the beginning.

BLS: And you knew each other for a long time before you married, right?

Alene: We met in January of 1972, and we married on August 16, 1983. It was a long courtship! [laughs]

BLS: Long enough for you to discover the foibles of each, and yet you still chose to get married.

Alene: Yes, and we were right. I think we did just great.

Dan: Oh, yes. This was the second marriage for both of us.

I had been married briefly at the age of 45 to Elizabeth Hatcher. Alene had also been married, and she has a son and daughter from that marriage.

BLS: So you have now been married for 16 years.

Alene: That's right. And we've known each other for 27 years. It will be 28 years in January.

BLS: It looks like you might make it, doesn't it?

Alene: I have a feeling we're going to! [laughs] I keep thinking, "If he'll just behave now ..."

Dan: I try!

BLS: Well, when I first met Dan, he commented, "I think Alene has the most beautiful smile I've ever seen."

Alene: Oh, thank you! He's a kind person, and he never wants to hurt anybody's feelings. And he doesn't say, "Do this." Some men will say, "Do this, do that." Dan says, "If you get time, would you do such and such? And if you don't get time today, how about tomorrow?"

Alene and her granddaughter, Christina, at Easter.

And he has such a wonderful sense of humor. If I start to get mad, he'll say something that's funny, and then I can't get mad! He has been a wonderful husband.

Dan: Thank you. You're a wonderful wife … so we're even!

Alene: Every woman ought to have the opportunity to have a good husband like Dan. But I'm not going to share him with her! One thing that really surprised me about Dan was that he just fell into marriage as though he'd been married all his life. I was shocked. After all, he was 70 years old when we got married. Marriage must really agree with him!

Is there anything you would like to say about our relationship for the last 27 years, Dan?

Dan: Well … it's great! [laughs]

Alene: Dan never would let me cut our wedding cake. We still have that cake—it's in the freezer. I was going to cut it on our wedding day, but he said: "No, let's don't cut it. Let's wait until tomorrow or the next day." Later he said, "Let's save it until our first anniversary, and then we'll cut it." So on our first anniversary I asked, "Do you want a piece of cake?" He said, "No, I don't believe so"!

Alene decorates the house lavishly for children and adults alike to enjoy during Christmas season.

About a week or two before our tenth anniversary—this is so sweet—he started telling me, "Let's dress up in the clothes that we got married in and have our picture made." I said: "Oh, yeah. Which leg do you want me to wear my dress on?" [laughs] I'd put on about ten pounds by then. I just kept laughing about that—but he was serious!

On the morning of our anniversary, he said, "I asked Bill Steele to come down here and take some pictures of us in our wedding clothes." I said, "Dan, are you serious?" He said: "Yes. He's going to be here at three o'clock." So I got out my dress, and I had to let the seams out! We got dressed, and Sondra got the cake out of the freezer and put it back together. So we had pictures made with our wedding cake, in the same clothes that we got married in, on our tenth anniversary.

The cake is still in the freezer. It's probably petrified. I finally decided that it's become an antique and we will have to sell it! [laughs] I guess next year I'm going to have to bring it out on our anniversary and take a picture.

Dan: Yes, I think so.

Alene: We could get new clothes!

Dan and Alene were married on August 16, 1983, after an 11 year courtship.

Dan with his niece, Catherine Ann.

Three generations of Stowe men: Young Allan, Harding, Richmond, Dan, Harding Jr., Robert Lee.

Dan with his sister, Catherine Pharr.

Starting Traditions of Our Own

Christmas at my parents' house was always such a wonderful time for the whole family. In recent years, Alene and I have enjoyed creating our own holiday traditions here at Seven Oaks Farm.

When interviewed separately by the editor, Harding Stowe and Catherine Ann Carstarphen shared their responses to the Stowe holiday traditions for this generation:

Harding: We used to go to McAdenville maybe once a year, usually for Thanksgiving. My aunt, Catherine Pharr, hosted Thanksgiving for as long as she was able, and then her daughter, Catherine Ann, hosted it for a while. That has splintered up a bit, though. We haven't been able to do that recently. So Dan's big Christmas extravaganza has really been the family social event.

BLS: For how many years?

Harding: At least 15 years—maybe longer. I remember going before our daughter was born, and she's 14 now. It's been a very, very nice tradition. It means as much to my children, I think, as Santa Claus coming or anything else we do at Christmas. Dan and Alene do a first-class job of trying to make it a really nice occasion for everyone. And they have a magnificent place for hosting the gathering.

Catherine Ann: Christmas at Dan's is like going to a fairyland! [laughs] It is absolutely enchanting. From the moment you walk through the door, the decorations and music are beautiful. Alene and Dan are wonderful, gracious hosts.

Dan and Robert Lee exchange Christmas gifts with Young Allan, son of Harding Stowe, and Alexandra, daughter of Martin Carstarphen.

The Wives and Mothers

Carol Carstarphen, wife to Bill Pharr, married August 24, 1989.

Becky Stowe, wife of Richmond, married May 14, 1994.

Lisa Carstarphen, wife of Martin, married March 17, 1989.

Pam Stowe, wife of Harding, married June 19, 1982.

Chris Stowe, wife of Robert Lee, married January 15, 1983.

Dan with Harding Jr.

Christmas picture of the grandnieces and -nephews: Catherine Stowe Pharr Henderson, daughter of Catherine S. P. Carstarphen; Johnathan Wood Carstarphen, son of Carol and Bill Pharr Carstarphen; Alexandra Pharr Carstarphen, daughter of Lisa and Martin Carstarphen; Isabel Bannister Carstarphen, daughter of Lisa and Martin Carstarphen; Joseph Benjamin Carstarphen, son of Carol and Bill Pharr Carstarphen; William James Pharr Carstarphen, Jr., son of Carol and Bill Pharr Carstarphen. (Courtesy of Catherine Ann Carstarphen.)

There is everything in the world for the children. The family includes Uncle Robert's children and grandchildren, and my children and grandchildren. So there are a lot of little children at the party, and Dan makes them feel welcome. Each year he tries to get a different toy that they'll all enjoy playing with—fascinating things. And for the last two years, he has given them each a keepsake. Two years ago the little girls got lockets, and last year they were each given a charm bracelet. He also shows a Christmas movie on his wide, film screen.

Catherine Ann's granddaughter, Alexandra, enjoys the toys Dan and Alene provide for the children at the Stowe Christmas party.

Dan with Young Allan Stowe, son of Harding and Pam Stowe.

The Stowe family grandchildren (not pictured: Hannah, daughter of Richmond, born in February): (Front row, left to right) Bennett, daughter of Richmond Stowe; Isabel, daughter of Martin Carstarphen; Jonathan, son of Bill Pharr Carstarphen. (Second row, left to right) Catherine, daughter of Catherine S.P. Carstarphen; Young Allan, son of Harding Stowe; Benjamin, son of Bill Pharr; William James Pharr, son of Bill Pharr Carstarphen. (Fourth row, left to right) Lillian, daughter of Robert Lee Stowe; Christine, daughter of Robert Lee Stowe; Harding Jr., son to Harding Stowe; Alexandra, daughter to Martin Carstarphen. (Fifth row) Palmer, daughter of Harding Stowe.

The oldest "grandchild," Palmer Stowe, with her mother, Pam, wife of Harding Stowe.

Dan and Alene have a sled that they put outside. Several years, it has snowed as we are coming out or going in—not a whole lot, but just enough to excite the children even more. The children always get on that sled before they go home.

It's a seven o'clock party, so we eat dinner there. The meal is wonderful and gorgeous. After dinner, Alene always has a game for the children. It will be a little box or a puzzle, and if you can get it open, there's a treasure such as a gold coin on the inside— something that's just lots of fun. The children feel like they've died and gone to heaven! [laughs] They think a lot of Great-Uncle Dan.

Alene is a gracious hostess. She has so many children to buy gifts for, but every toy she selects is something that they really like. It's usually the newest toy. That is the child's present, aside from all of the other keepsakes and little games and candy.

It takes a lot of work to put on a party like that—and to make it one that all ages will enjoy. Alene and Dan do a wonderful job of making everybody feel welcome. It's just a beautiful, fun party. It makes Christmas for us.

Works Cited

Cope, Robert F., and Wellman, Manly Wade. County of Gaston. Gaston County Historical Society: 1961.

Ragan, Robert A. The Pioneer Cotton Mills in Gaston County: 1848-1904.

Editor:
Beth Laney Smith

While dancing, Richmond dips his daughter, Bennett, to give Uncle Robert Lee a big Christmas smile.

Newest addition to the Stowe family, Hannah, daughter of Richmond and Becky, was born February 23, 2000.

Robert Lee's daughters, Christine and Lillian Stowe.

Dan with the family of Robert Lee.

Chapter 3

Down on the Farm

"Buy land—because they aren't making any more of it."

—Dan Stowe

"Swans may look graceful, but they are sort of mean things. If you walk up to one, he'll stand there and look at you—and he might even bite you!"

"We just don't have enough land."

In 1901, at about the time he went into the textile business in Belmont, my father bought an 82-acre farm in the South Point area. Our family resided on North Main Street from the time I was four years old, and though we never lived on that farm, my daddy took me there often. Even as a small boy, I loved to ride out there and see the beauty and expanse of the property. From these happily spent afternoons came my desire to own a house in the country one day. I would comment to my daddy, "We need something like this—with more land. We just don't have enough land at home!"

My father once confided, "I know that if I don't succeed in the textile business, I can run the farm to make a living." He was thankful that he never had to do that, because the

textile industry became his passion. But while I developed a deep respect and appreciation for my father's business sense, land and its preservation always appealed to me more. I would have loved growing up on a farm. Something deep inside of me responded to all of those rolling acres.

I still believe that one should never get too far from the land. We are all tied to it somewhere. I truly feel sorry for people who do not have the opportunity to spend any significant time with the land. They miss something.

By age four or five, I was accompanying my father on drives along South Point Road. The road in that area circled around so that we never had to turn back in order to go home. Instead we would continue traveling forward and eventually end up back where we had started. We called this "going around the loop." It was during these 15-mile expeditions that I caught my first glimpse of the old McLean house and what had once been its slave quarters. Years later I would purchase that property and build my own home nearby.

"All really grim gardeners possess a keen sense of humus."
— W.C. Sellar and R.J. Yeatman,
Garden Rubbish

Left to right: Cora Lee McCorkle, Charles Irwin McCorkle, Dan, and Roy Turner. Mr. McCorkle was the farm manager, and he and his wife lived on the premises for many years. Turner's daughters, Sondra Schronce and Vicki Funderberk, are respectively the housekeeper and the cook at Seven Oaks Farm today.

No Better Place Than Belmont

I have always felt that the South Fork area is where I belong. While I have done my share of traveling, and enjoy vacationing in the mountains and at the beach, I cannot imagine being content anywhere else for very long. So when I began to seriously consider purchasing land of my own, Belmont was naturally my first choice.

As a young man, I was very interested in boating, so I found riverside property especially appealing. Seven Oaks Farm, where I have made my home for more than 30 years, is situated on a peninsula almost surrounded by water. The nearby South Fork River is visible from my bedroom and living room windows.

J. B. Holcomb shows off an enormous cabbage from the farm's garden.

I acquired my first piece of property on December 4, 1941, when I was 28 years old. The deed established the purchase of 390 acres of land in the South Fork area from Martin Farms. My father was very supportive of this venture, not only morally but financially. He put up some mill stock as collateral, and thus I was able to secure a loan to purchase the property. In fact, I have borrowed money for all my land purchases. I paid off these debts with a great sense of satisfaction as I earned money. After all, land does not wear out or become obsolete.

Just days after my initial acquisition, my attention turned—along with that of the rest of the world—to graver matters. On December 7, the bombing of Pearl Harbor by the Japanese took the lives of 2,330 U.S. servicemen. An additional 1,145 were wounded, and there were 100 civilian casualties. As a result, the United States was brought into alliance with China, and I knew I would soon be called to military service. I decided to take enlistment matters into my own hands and applied for the U.S. Navy shortly thereafter. I was notified of my acceptance in April of 1942. Meanwhile, on April 21, I closed the purchase of 5.14 acres from J. A. Armstrong. The following month I reported for duty, and my land-buying activities were curtailed until World War II ended.

At the time I joined the U.S. Navy needed officers with a college degree and business experience. I met both of these standards and was immediately made an ensign. Initially, I was stationed at the Mayport Section Base in Jacksonville, Florida, where I was assigned as the commanding officer of a patrol boat. It was a small craft, so I was joined by only six crew members. We patrolled areas along the coast, looking for German submarines. After about six months, I was promoted to naval operations in Charleston. Eventually I was transferred to Washington, D.C., and remained there until the end of the war.

Upon returning home from service in 1945, I renewed my pursuit of acquiring tracts of land. On October 31 of that year, I gained my next hundred acres from G. E. and Clemmie Mills McKee. Polly McLean Ragan sold me 200 acres on December 11, 1946. I bought 326 acres from Charles K. and Mary M. Bryant on April 16, 1947, and 19 more acres

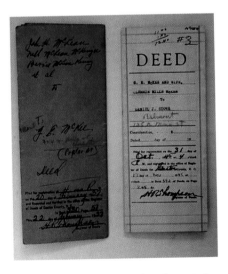

The deed transferring ownership of a tract of McLean land to G. E. McKee on February 20, 1937, and the deed for Dan's purchase of the same land on October 31, 1945. (By Steve Rankin Photography.)

from Martin Farms on April 1, 1949. Two years later, on July 3, S. L. Armstrong sold me 44.06 acres. My final acquisition was 37.5 acres from Duke Power Company on August 1, 1957. In less than 16 years, I had assembled almost 1,122 acres. My total investment was between $40,000 and $50,000.

Breathing Life Back Into the Soil

The property I acquired was in terrible shape. Cotton had been raised on it for a number of years, depleting the earth's nutrients. Severe erosion had created gullies as big as a house. I saw that before the land could be of any use, a lot of restoration was needed. So I sought advice from federal Soil and Water Conservation experts and went to work.

Because of the wide-scale erosion that had already begun, the primary concern was preventing the earth from washing into the Catawba River. Bulldozers were used to move soil into the gullies, making them more shallow. It took my farm crew an entire year to terrace the fields and seed them in Kentucky 31 fescue grass.

We also experimented with crop rotation and the integration of clover into the pastureland. Clover protects the earth from the erosion caused by wind and rain, and it naturally enriches the soil, furnishing nutrients for the grass. This meant we didn't have to depend as much on chemical fertilizers.

Alene gathers fresh greens from the garden.

Most often, the fence posts we used on this land were concrete rather than the wooden or treated types. Concrete posts last considerably longer, and they do not have the chemicals that are applied to treated posts. I never liked the idea of preservatives from the posts seeping down into the earth.

On September 22, 1989, Hurricane Hugo tore through the Carolinas, destroying houses, taking down large numbers of trees, and leaving a trail of debris in its wake. Dan ran a sawmill on his farm for almost a year in order to clear away fallen trees.

"We waited until it was almost dark to turn the turkeys loose, so that they would settle down and get used to the place before morning," Dan recalled. "Unfortunately, the turkeys had ideas of their own. I watched this one take off, and he never even slowed down. He went right on across the river!"

Running 1,200 acres takes a lot of help. In addition to myself and the farm manager, there were many different schoolboys who worked off and on at the farm over the years. And we all stayed busy. I found out that Dan really likes fresh, homegrown vegetables, so I always tried to keep his kitchen stocked with them. The tomato plants were difficult to grow, but we had better luck with other vegetables. We did a lot of mowing and back-hedging, too. Occasionally I delivered furniture for the Plantation House, which was Dan's antique shop.

Sometimes Dan would ask me to drive him up to the mountains or other places, and he sent me to check on things at his two vacation homes every now and then.

When Dan wanted to do something, such as build a fence, he would think it over and study it carefully. He always had some sort of project in the back of his mind. But it isn't hard to see

Animal Farm

Filling in the sparse vegetation with fescue grass not only anchored the earth in place, but it also allowed us to later run beef cattle on the property. For a time, we experimented with raising dairy cows there, but eventually we returned to beef cattle. Altogether, we ran cattle on the property for 40 years.

We also raised chickens and turkeys. Our chicken population grew to 4,000 laying hens, which yielded about 3,000 eggs a day. Regional hospitals bought many of these eggs.

Helping Hands

J. B. Holcomb was my property manager for 16 years, from 1972 until his retirement in 1988. His recollections of those years give a good general picture of life on the farm, where there was always something interesting—and sometimes even humorous—happening.

I was invited to escort a lady to a Christmas party at the McAdenville mill, and that was where I met Dan. Sometime after that, Eb Phillips, the caretaker of Seven Oaks, passed away, and I heard that Dan was looking for someone to fill his position. So I went over to Dan's house and met with him, and he gave me the job.

that of all of the things he has done, marrying Alene was one of the best things Dan ever did for himself.

The farm manager was Charles Irwin McCorkle, and he took care of the horses and cattle. He and his wife, Cora Lee, lived on the farm in the caretaker's house. Charles has passed away, and Cora Lee now lives in Gastonia. I've heard that Dan has remodeled the interior of the caretaker's house, although the exterior remains the same. Dan doesn't let anything go to waste. He takes care of things.

There are still cattle and horses on the farm. I don't know if there are any riding horses, but Dan used to love to ride. And wildlife is important to him. Dan enjoyed seeing the geese and ducks out near the water, so the other workers and I fed them every morning. I would count up to 90 of them and finally stop counting. The birds would rest and feed there as they migrated north or south.

There have been a few dogs at Seven Oaks. Dan liked to have a dog follow along when he took walks. One was a wild dog that had been running around near the Plantation House and bothering customers. Nell Stowe called me one day to come get it. I was going to take it to the pound, but I put a chain around its neck and got it over to the house, and after a

while the dog got to where it was used to me. I named it Alice—after making sure that was okay with Alice Conner. I have never seen a dog that could tree raccoons the way Alice could! There was also a beautiful chocolate lab, which used to run around, tearing through the landscaping by the side of the house that faces the river. Eventually we had to get rid of that one.

For a while, we had a problem with foxes. They got every last one of our chickens. Dan had some wild turkeys brought in—maybe 25 of them—and the foxes got those, too. I put those turkeys out and never saw them again.

Cora Lee McCorkle, a woman of diverse talents—many of them farm-related.

"As for what concerns the service of the king, for which you have sent me, Monsieur Le Comte, it is of the greatest interest for performing it to have a station in the center of a country the most interesting of all of America, that is to say Georgia, South Carolina, and North Carolina, . . ."

— André Michaux, in a letter written in
Charleston, S.C., and addressed to
Charles-Claude De La Billarderie, comte D'Angiviller.
November 12, 1786.

"It's a good thing I like English peas."

Dan used to have a houseboat docked down at the river. I would guess it was about 54 feet long. To my knowledge, he didn't ever stay on that particular boat overnight, but he and Bill Pharr did take it out on the river. I would go along and steer. This was very difficult at times, because the wind could really blow on a boat that size.

Dan once owned a 1931 Ford coupe, and it was a one-seater. He needed to take some gas down to one of his boats one time, so he had a man who worked for him sit in the rumble seat with a five-gallon can of gas while Dan drove the car. From the way Dan told the story, he must have really taken off and gone flying down that gravel road. The man got out to leave the can of gas, but instead of getting back into the car, he said, "No sir, Mr. Stowe—I'm walking back!"

From McLean Quarters to Seven Oaks Farm

Much of the land I accumulated over the years had once been owned by Dr. William McLean (1757-1828) and later by his son, Dr. John Davidson McLean (1794-1880). Their property was known as the McLean Quarters. A farm was already in operation on the land when Andre Michaux, the legendary botanical explorer, came through this area. Michaux, botanist to Louis XVI of France, arrived in New York in November 1785 and spent 11 years traveling

through North America, collecting and studying the indigenous plants.[1] He kept a very detailed journal of his travels, wherein he mentioned passing by the William McLean house.[2]

Dr. John McLean owned over 1,300 acres in South Point Township at the time of his death on November 27, 1880.[3] The section of the McLean Quarters where he and his family lived was known as the Houston Place, because it

---

[1] Savage: p. 4, 34.
[2] Bill Steele, DSBG director of development, Daniel Stowe Botanical Garden
[3] Gaston County Superior Court, Will Book 3, p. 145

had been owned previously by Thomas Houston. According to local legend, Thomas and his kin were closely related to the famous Sam Houston, who served as governor of both Tennessee and Texas. However, this claim is not supported by research of Sam Houston's genealogy.[4]

The Catawba Power Company dammed up the Catawba River in 1901,[5] creating what is now known as Lake Wylie—and putting much of the McLeans' very valuable land under water.[6] Today, the Catawba Power Company is known as Duke Energy.

Meanwhile, ownership of the Houston Place passed through the hands of several members of the McLean family. John Davidson Brevard McLean (1852-1936), who was a son of Dr. John D. McLean and his second wife, Martha Edith Bigger McLean, bought the tract from his own son, Charles, on March 24, 1915.[7]

It was during his residence in the old McLean house on the Houston Place that the name of that particular tract was changed to Seven Oaks. According to McLean family sources, it was John D. B. McLean's daughter Nell who came up with the appellation, in honor of the seven large oaks that surrounded the house at that time.[8] For me, the words "Seven Oaks" have become synonymous with home.

Farmer Dan commanding his Ford 4600 tractor.

Works Cited

The following sources were compiled by Alice Conner in a historical sketch on the McLean house:

> Armstrong, Zella. Notable Southern Families. Baltimore. ©1974.
>
> Gaston County Register of Deeds, Book 105.
>
> Gaston County Superior Court, Will Book 3.
>
> Interview with Mrs. L. L. McLean, May 1986.

Additional works cited:

> Maynor, Joe. *Duke Power: The First Seventy-Five Years.* Delmar.
>
> Pettus, Louise. *A Roddey Family.* 1998.
>
> Savage, Henry, Jr., and Elizabeth J. *André and Francois André Michaux.* The University Press of Virginia: Charlottesville, Va. ©1986.

Editor:
Beth Laney Smith

---

[4]Armstrong, p. 179
[5]Pettus: pp. 38-39
[6]Maynor: p.21
[7]Gaston County Register of Deeds, Book 105, p. 473
[8]Interview with Mrs. L. L. McLean, May 1986.

All of the above photographs by Rick Haithcox Photography.

Chapter 4

McAdenville:
A Village of Lights

1881-1939

Dan joined the U.S. Navy in 1942 and was commissioned an ensign. He was later promoted to lieutenant.

Robert Lee Stowe, Sr. (Courtesy of Ermintrude Little Mullen.)

For want of a job, a young man set in motion a chain of events that would revitalize one of North Carolina's most historic and prominent mill villages. To bring this about, it was necessary to combine his vision with the financial acumen of his father, Robert Lee Stowe, and the textile expertise of his brother-in-law, William J. Pharr. This combination of talents and experience resulted in a success story now legendary in the textile industry.

Dan Stowe's advocation of restoring the dormant McAden Mills to operation during the late 1930s may well be the first active example of his philosophy of the continuity of life, a deeply held conviction that one should incorporate the old into the new, thus preserving history for future generations.

William J. "Bill" Pharr. (Courtesy of Catherine Ann Pharr Carstarphen.)

Even in their early years, the lights were always the essence of the Christmas spirit. (By Steve Rankin Photography.)

in 1880 to Col. Rufus Yancey McAden, a Charlotte banker and railroad pioneer.

"Colonel McAden was an imposing, dynamic person in a time when hardly anybody in Gaston County or this area was," commented Gaston County historian Robert Ragan. "He was a director and organizer of some of the railroads that would become the Southern Railroad in 1894.

"My father, through his father, used to describe Colonel McAden's appearance. He dressed formally in a black frock coat and a tall, silk, top hat. He was prominent in the railroad, which was called the Atlanta and Charlotte Airline at that time. The railroad went through Lowell, and it came right by McAdenville but didn't actually come into town. But the train would stop for Colonel McAden, because of his connections with the railroad, to let him out when he came from Charlotte! He would get off the train in an open field, wearing his frock coat and silk hat, and walk some distance across the field to the mill office or store. That was a sight that was seldom seen in the Gaston County of the 1880s."

Colonel Rufus McAden was one of four incorporators of Springs Shoals Manufacturing Company. The others were his brother, John H. McAden; his son Benjamin T. McAden; and Jasper Stowe. At the time of his death in 1889, Rufus is believed to have been one of the wealthiest men in North Carolina.

Because of the preservation of its remarkable old buildings, McAdenville is considered an architectural treasure by many. Mill No. 2, with its dominating facade, is an excellent example of early efforts to erect buildings with more architectural embellishments than those of typical mill-village structures. Almost castle-like in its appearance, the building features twin corner turrets capped by copper roofs. The bell tower's second cupola, pictured here, is no longer in existence. (By Steve Rankin Photography.)

The Birth Of an Enterprise

Originally named Springs Shoals Manufacturing Company, this McAdenville organization was the sixth cotton mill in Gaston County.[1] It was established in 1881 on lands owned by the heirs of Adam Alexander Springs, overlooking the South Fork River. Sometime after Springs' death in about 1840, the tract of land had been acquired by William A. and Jasper Stowe, distant relatives of Dan. The Stowe brothers sold the land, now known as McAdenville,

The mill interior, circa 1939.

The basic needs of the mill workers were met locally. Around the original mill were a cotton gin and press, a wheat mill, and a corn mill. These had been built by Ben McAden prior to the construction of Springs Shoals Manufacturing. The local general store, McAden & Ragan, which operated in connection with the mill, carried groceries, notions, dry goods, and farm implements. The store was a gathering place for people throughout the area. Mill employees were paid in cardboard money called "scrip," which could be used at McAden & Ragan to buy everything from food and clothing to coffins and nails. Rows of brick mill houses stood nearby. These charming homes had hardwood floors, and it is said that the bricks used for the exterior walls were made on site by prison labor.[2] The bricks are richly textured and appear quite obviously handmade.

[1] Ragan: *The Pioneer Cotton Mills of Gaston County (N.C.).*
[2] Miller: p. 31.

The company checks for Stowe Mills, Inc., featured this rendering of Mill No. 2. (By Steve Rankin Photography.)

It is believed that Thomas Edison himself traveled to McAdenville in 1884 to install the first electric generator in an American textile mill. The generator's source of energy was the river, and initially it was used only to power the mill's lighting. It is said that the Edison generator Number 31 ran for 80 years.[3]

People came from hundreds of miles around, in buggies and on horseback, to view McAden Mills' incandescent lights, the first in any southern mill. Electric lights meant the mill could run 24 hours a day.

A close-up of the bell tower and cupola, as they appear today.

"My grandfather, George Washington Ragan, remembered when the first electric lights were installed in the mill," said Robert Ragan. "In the summertime, they would have a party up on the hill overlooking the factory to watch as the beautiful lights came on. The local people called them 'lights in a bottle.'"

After its construction, the mill—and in turn the picturesque town of McAdenville—flourished. Indeed, McAdenville quickly became an important trading center in Gaston County.

A second charter was issued in 1883. This charter included two important points: the name of Springs Shoals Manufacturing Company was officially changed to McAden Mills, and the town of McAdenville was incorporated. The company's new name was plural even though it remained a single plant until Mill No. 2 was constructed in 1884 and 1885. The four original incorporators were listed on the new charter, with the addition of Henry M. McAden, another of Rufus' sons.

By early 1884, McAden Mills was the largest textile plant in Gaston County. It established a long-lasting economic foundation for both North and South Carolina, feeding future transportation, chemical, and banking industries. At that time, McAden Mills produced 3,000 pounds of yarns and warps daily and employed over 100 people. During the next 50 years, it expanded to include three plants, containing 28,000 spindles and 350 looms.

Restored carding machines, circa 1939. The mill's posts, some of which are visible in the background, are made of heart pine. Popular because of its durability, that type of wood was no longer available in this region after about 1900, because the trees were cut down for building purposes. (Courtesy of Steve Rankin Archives.)

[3]Ragan: *The Pioneer Cotton Mills of Gaston County (N.C.).*

The original bridge on the South Fork River, which eventually deteriorated and was replaced by the R. L. Stowe Bridge in 1948. (Courtesy of Steve Rankin Archives.)

Another view of the original bridge. This photo captures the catastrophic flood of 1916. A group of men is gathered at the other end of the bridge, surveying the swollen river. (Courtesy of Steve Rankin Archives.)

Restoring salvageable machinery to working condition took many hours of hard labor. Fortunately, many mill workers were skilled mechanics who were able to pinpoint and correct the problems. The men shown here are repairing a carding machine. Most of the mill's equipment was either obsolete or in poor shape by the time Dan, his father, and Bill Pharr bought the mill. Some machines were reconditioned and others were replaced before the mill could begin running again. (Courtesy of Steve Rankin Archives.)

The first telephone system in Gaston County was built in McAdenville during the 1880s by Henry M. McAden, who at that time was in his teens. The system consisted of only two telephones, running from the McAdens' home to the mill office. McAdenville also had the first library in Gaston County, built in 1906 and endowed to the town by Dr. Giles M. McAden, in memory of his father, Rufus. The building is still preserved.

Mill No. 2 was built in 1884 and 1885. During the later stages of construction, the center of the building's front was capped with a grand, impressive bell tower. Medieval-looking, turreted towers were added to define the frontmost left and right corners. (See photo, page 46.) Sometime during the 1890s, the bell tower's cupola was toppled by a storm. It was replaced by a new cupola with a completely different design.[4]

Power for the plant's machinery was supplied in the early years by the nearby South Fork River. Between the time McAden Mills opened in 1881 and the flood of 1916, the mills operated continuously, except when the river was low in the summer or frozen over in the winter. During the winter of 1893, ice formed so thickly on the pond that it was cut into blocks and stored to use in the summer. Dependency on the river was finally eliminated in 1909, when commercial electric power became available in the area.

The South Fork overran its banks frequently, but the 1916 flood was a singularly devastating event. The flood put the plant under water, nearly demolishing it. Many employees were forced to evacuate their homes, and they remained out of work until the mills could be restored to running condition.

The creation of highways 29 and 74 in 1927 established a direct link from Gastonia to Charlotte, which brought significantly more business for McAden Mills. Increasingly, commercial trucks replaced horse-and-wagon delivery.

---

[4] Miller: p.50.

They picked up machinery, parts, and raw material from train depots, and were often used in the shipment of finished yarn.

By then, McAdenville was a typical Piedmont mill village with a school, churches, and even a brass band. Activities such as baseball were organized to provide wholesome recreation for the mill hands after their long workdays. It has been said that McAden Mills' treasurer and general manager, Robert R. Ray, would not hire a man unless he could play baseball, so McAdenville always had a strong team.[5]

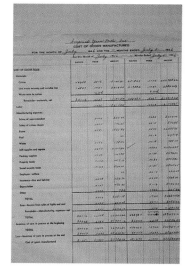

A page from the 1946 journal for Imperial Yarn Mills, Inc. (By Steve Rankin Photography.)

Pictured here before its renovation, this McAdenville house is currently being used as the mill's personnel offices. At one time it was the residence of the McAden family. The house had marble sinks and the first bathtub in Gaston County. (Courtesy of the Gaston County Historic Properties Commission.)

ties, religious views, and ways of thinking. Although life in the noisy, lint-filled mills was hard, the sense of community, with its shared concerns and experiences, was a source of solace, support, and even joy. Thus, sticking together—lending a quilt, bartering for goods, gathering at square dances—meant the difference between enjoying life and merely enduring.

Exterior of the personnel office building after restoration. Some of the interior floors remain on a slant, which is a common occurrence among older houses. (Courtesy of the Gaston County Historic Properties Commission.)

McAdenville and its mills proved to be starting points for many influential men in Gaston County. George Alexander Gray and George Washington Ragan started at McAden Mills and went on to become two of the most prominent textile manufacturers in the South. Dr. L. N. Glenn set up his medical practice in McAdenville, then founded the City Hospital in Gastonia. Samuel N. Boyce began as a bookkeeper at the mill and later became a prominent banker in Gastonia. Another early bookkeeper was W. T. Love, who also became a textile manufacturer. Rufus P. Rankin was a McAdenville merchant before he went into textiles and banking.

The paternalistic model of management, brought to the South from the mills of New England, created a cooperative culture with unique customs, folklore, activi-

---

[5] Miller: p.39.

A railway siding ran between the two plants to facilitate delivery of raw materials and shipment of finished yarn.

This unity proved to be crucial. In 1935, during the middle of the Great Depression, McAden Mills shut down, because there was no one to buy the yarn they produced. A union dispute also contributed to the closing. The mills would remain inactive for four years. McAdenville had never known any industry but textiles, so the closing of McAden Mills was an enormous hardship for the townspeople.

Fortunately, in 1939, three enterprising partners took the initiative to get wheels turning and paychecks into hands of the residents. Robert Lee Stowe, Dan Stowe, and William J. Pharr purchased and renovated the mills against expert advice. Thus McAden Mills became Stowe Mills, Inc. The partners also acquired the town property in the transaction.

Since the original establishment of the mills, concern for workers and their families had always been a priority for management. The strong sense of community that had carried McAdenville's residents through hard times would be bolstered in upcoming years by the involvement of the Pharr and Stowe families.

As happened in 1881, the textile company once again became the lifeblood of McAdenville. Stowe Mills, Inc.— and later its subsidiaries, Pharr Worsted and Pharr Yarns— was a phenomenal success. Here, Dan picks up the narrative in his own words.

Left to right: W. J. Pharr, Maxine Smith Goins, Thelma McClure, Florine Pressley, Ilena Pratt, and Dan Stowe. (Courtesy of Steve Rankin Archives.)

I Get a Job

After my education at Davidson, I studied for about a year at King's Business School (now known as King's College) in Charlotte. I finished there in 1936. Then I worked at the Chronicle Mill office in Belmont for about a year, while my brother, Robert Lee, Jr., who was 11 years older than me, ran Belmont Hosiery Mills.

I was pretty far behind my brother in terms of experience within my father's companies. Papa believed one of the best ways for me to catch up was to encounter all aspects of the business. One of the first things he did was to send me out to sell yarn. I remember the time he sent me up north to see a customer in Philadelphia. The Depression was on then. The customer was an old gentleman, and he was especially nice to me. He treated me as if I were his best friend, and he bought an order. He was the first customer to whom I personally sold an order. I'll always remember him. He gave me a lot of confidence. And that's why Papa had sent me up there—to get a lesson in selling by doing it myself.

Papa was always very good about helping me along with things, so I told him I'd like to see if we could find something else for me to do. I had heard that McAden Mills had been closed for several years and was for sale, so I talked to him about it. My father wasn't too interested right at first, but he started delving into it. His reluctance was understandable, because the physical condition of McAden Mills at that time was not good. It was a decrepit plant full of rusty, outdated machinery. One Philadelphia yarn broker called it "the biggest pile of junk you ever saw."

Many friends, associates, and financiers couldn't imagine why we'd be interested in such a rundown place. But my father saw potential. After looking at several options, he began making plans to buy the mills and the village. He estimated purchase, restoration, operation, and maintenance costs to be about $250,000, a tremendous amount of money in 1936. At the time, my father was 71 years old.

Before long, he had the details pretty well worked out. Several of his friends joined him in putting down money to purchase the mills and the surrounding town of 450 acres. The original shareholders—the McAden family—maintained a percentage. The Henry Belk family also owned a

The program of events from the dedication of the R. L. Stowe Bridge in McAdenville on November 18, 1948. (By Steve Rankin Photography.)

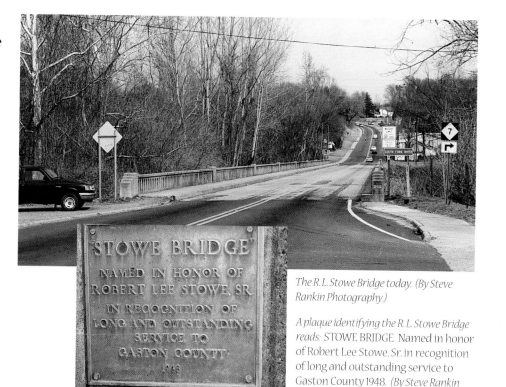

The R. L. Stowe Bridge today. (By Steve Rankin Photography.)

A plaque identifying the R. L. Stowe Bridge reads: STOWE BRIDGE Named in honor of Robert Lee Stowe, Sr. in recognition of long and outstanding service to Gaston County 1948. (By Steve Rankin Photography.)

percentage. Of the controlling interest, my father owned a third and I owned a third. The remaining third was owned by William J. Pharr, who had married my sister Catherine in 1927. Thus Stowe Mills, Inc., was established, and McAden Mills returned to operation under this new name. The Belmont Land Investment Company was also formed at that time, serving as the real estate holding company for the McAdenville property.

This certificate from the first annual Community Day on July 7, 1951, guaranteed its bearer a plateful of tasty barbecue. Among the day's featured events were a "battle of the sexes" ball game, a greased pole climb, a greased-pig catching contest, boxing bouts, and a men's egg-throwing contest. (Courtesy of the Daniel J. Stowe Foundation, Inc.)

My dad traveled to Washington, D.C., several times by train. There he visited the Reconstruction Finance Corporation (RFC), which was established to help small businesses with operating expenses. The RFC granted us a $135,000 loan to restore the mills. The mills and town property, which we had already purchased, were used as collateral.

On May 11, 1939, I walked over to the headquarters building with the keys and unlocked the door to the office. As far as mill equipment went, we had to junk practically everything. The machinery was in a bad state of repair—nothing had been modernized over the years—and we took sledgehammers to it. At that time there was a spur

line from the P&N Railroad that went right down to the mills. We got rid of carload after carload of waste, and put in good second-hand machinery and spinning equipment. Previously the mills had produced cloth, but we were not fabric makers—we were spinners. So the looms were broken apart and hauled off with the rest of the old machinery.

In October 1939, the first bale of cotton went through the mill and came out as yarn. From then on, the plant ran day and night. It immediately started taking off and doing well, because we made a yarn nobody else

Special guests at the 50th anniversary celebration included: (first row, left to right) Catherine Ann Pharr Carstarphen, Catherine Stowe Pharr, Dan Stowe, and Alene Stowe; (second row) Ilena Pratt and Robert "Buck" Rector. (By Steve Rankin Photography.)

was making. Ours was a coarse yarn, which was useful in producing army goods and other heavy materials, while everybody else was making fine yarns. We also made carded and combed yarns. And the economy in general was improving.

I was named secretary, assistant treasurer, and director of Stowe Mills. Bill was made vice president and director. Prior to his position there, he had been the superintendent of two mills in Belmont, so he knew the business from sweeping the floors on up. He knew everything. I learned a lot from him and, fortunately, from being in the right place at the right time. I was lucky to work with him and my father.

Years later, many of the older hands would recollect that Bill often walked out into the plant with them, put his arm around them, and told them he appreciated the job they were doing. Everyone called him "Mr. Bill." Later, he became mayor of McAdenville and sat on the county board of commissioners. He was a true leader.

In 1963, upon the death of my father, Bill Pharr was made president of the company, and he served as its dynamic leader until his death in 1981. At that time, I became the president.

In order to show appreciation to local law enforcement officers, Stowe Mills entertained the entire group at Dan's property on the lake one day each year. Dan, in his early thirties, is seated at the far right behind the first row, wearing his yachtsman's cap. Also among the group are Bill Pharr, seated third from the right in the first row, and Henry Lineberger, seated at the far right of the same row. (By Steve Rankin Photography.)

Improvements Made by Stowe Mills in McAdenville

One of the first things Stowe Mills did for the town was to install running water. The water was pumped from deep wells to the back porches of the homes. Indoor plumbing came at a later date.[6] We also renovated the mill houses that had fallen into disrepair and built some new ones.

The war started not too long after that. This was unfortunate for our nation, but it helped the mill get back on its feet. As soon as that war started, boy, everything went to town! We made enough yarn for many of our servicemen's uniforms and sold a lot to a factory in Greenville, South Carolina. I hate to mention the fact that the war helped us!

After serving in the U.S. Navy from 1942 through 1945, I recuperated from an unrelated health problem but kept active in the operation of Stowe Mills. Any time a decision was made, if I wasn't at the mill, someone would call me on the phone and we'd discuss whether to go ahead with this or that.

Dan enjoys the company of two other naval officers during his days in the service.

In 1946 I resumed my full duties at Stowe Mills. The GIs brought skills back with them from the war; there wasn't anything they couldn't rig up. Right at the end of the war, a man named Dayton Larzerlere came to us with the idea of running wool on cotton mill machinery. That had never been done before. We had some really good craftsmen around the mill, and they altered the machinery to where we could indeed run wool on cotton machines. Cotton is about an inch and an eighth or so a staple, but you could get wool in almost any length you wanted. So we had to adjust the rollers, setting them wide apart, to take care of that. Then when nylon came along, it ran on the same rollers—but we could make it any length we wanted to, because it was extruded. We were the first to spin nylon on cotton machinery.

In 1945, Stowe Mills began a diversification program, starting with the successful experimentation of spinning worsted yarn on our cotton machinery. It turned out to be as high quality as that produced by the existing worsted machinery. Pharr Worsted Mills, Inc., was formed as a subsidiary, with the same officers as Stowe Mills.

In 1950, we pioneered the production of synthetic yarn with modified machinery, resulting in the formation of another new subsidiary, Pharr Yarns, Inc. By mid 1960, cotton was totally phased out of all of our mills in favor of synthetic yarn. The company now manufactures synthetic yarn for sweaters, hosiery, carpeting, and more. They also produce high-performance yarns for fire prevention and cut-resistant materials.

In 1956, Pharr Yarns purchased the closed Spencer Mountain Mills and village from Duke Power Company and began renovations. By then, we were old hands at modernizing textile plants.

During the 1960 to 1970 period, Pharr acquired a number of other mill companies in the area. These included the Imperial, Sterling, and Crescent mills in Belmont. In the late 1980s, the company also acquired United Spinners in Lowell. Through a series of mergers, these companies

This festively decorated cake was the centerpiece of the refreshment table. (By Steve Rankin Photography.)

[6] Miller: p. 97.

Dan was joined by two special ladies—his longtime secretary, Ilena Pratt, and his sister, Catherine Pharr—for this photograph, taken at Stowe-Pharr's 50th anniversary celebration. Mrs. Pratt (center) worked for the company for 50 years.

were combined into Pharr, and on March 28, 1992, Pharr and Stowe were merged into one company—Stowe-Pharr Mills. This followed the consolidation in 1990 of the ownership of the company within the Pharr/Carstarphen family.

The McAdenville Foundation and Baseball

Stowe Mills set up the privately funded McAdenville Foundation in the 1950s, and arranged for the construction of a community center with a public swimming pool. We hired a director who organized athletic activities for the community's children. Now we have a full professional staff.

William James "Bill" Pharr, Jr., was born on April 26, 1930. He attended Belmont Abbey Preparatory School, and graduated from Davidson College in 1953. He was a textile executive with Stowe Mills, Pharr Yarns, and Pharr Worsted Mills, and was highly active in civic and community affairs in McAdenville, Spencer Mountain, and Gastonia. Bill married Laura Bryan Woodward Pharr on April 3, 1959, and they resided in Gastonia. He died on May 19, 1961, at the age of 31, after a battle with cancer. (By Steve Rankin Photography.)

Baseball was everybody's favorite pastime. McAdenville's slow-pitch softball team won its first National Tournament in 1960. It won again in 1961 and 1963.[7] Under the coaching of Doug McDonald, the McAdenville Reds won the tournament from 1970 to 1972, becoming the second team in the history of amateur softball (ASA) to earn three consecutive titles. The first team to do so was St. Louis, Missouri.

McAdenville's women set a softball record of their own. My sister, Catherine, believed the sport should not be confined to the men. So in the early 1960s, Bill Pharr approached Doug McDonald about setting up a ladies' team. The team was known as the McAdenville Redettes. It was only in existence for two seasons—from 1962 to

The mill's office workers got quite a surprise one day when a delivery truck driver lost control and his vehicle came crashing through the front of the building. Fortunately the office's occupant, Josh Chamberlin, had just gone to lunch. (By Steve Rankin Photography.)

1963—but placed second in the nation in its first year. After the Redettes folded, the town had plant league softball for women.[8]

The town's Fourth of July celebration always drew a lively crowd. The holiday was traditionally honored with special appearances by dignitaries and the performances of bands. Of course, we could never celebrate any occasion without the thrill of a good baseball game, so the great American pastime became an appropriate part of our Independence Day festivities.

---

[7] Miller, pg. 104.

[8] Doug McDonald

The recreation of the nativity beside the Baptist church reminds passers-by of the reason we celebrate Christmas. The scene is crowned by a "star," which seems to hover directly over the stable. (By Steve Rankin Photography.)

Christmastown, U.S.A.

But what put McAdenville on the national map was the Christmas light display. The idea actually originated after I put lights on some trees at our house in Belmont. At that time, I had recently built a small cabin on the Seven Oaks property, where the conservatory now stands. As Christmas approached, I put lights on several of the trees there, and my sister Catherine liked them so much that she decided the same should be done in McAdenville.

In December 1956, the McAdenville Men's Club asked Bill for permission to decorate nine trees in the area of the Community Center. Wayne Teague, a club member, said they wanted to create community spirit and liven the place up. Bill told them he would pay for the decorations if the Men's Club would put them up. The men planted more trees on Main Street and on roads that are visible nearby, just for this purpose. Each year, as the trees have grown, they have added more lights. Some of the trees are so large now that a cherry-picker is used to set up the display.

In 1980, when Christmastown, U.S.A., was featured on the Charles Kuralt show, we had more than 275 trees and 300,000 red, white, and green Christmas lights. Now every Christmas season, lights outline trees from the edge of town, down Main Street, around the lake, and beyond. The fountain in the middle is surrounded by colored lights.

Wayne Teague took over the installation of the lights. He and his crew have been installing them every year since 1957, with the McAdenville Foundation paying the December light bill. They start in August, checking how much wire and so forth they'll need. There are thousands of strings of lights. Then after Labor Day they spend five or six weeks making sure the bulbs work.

In October, the crew goes out and hangs lights, starting from the outside of the village and gradually moving in. They lay cables for the sound system, and hang wreaths and bows on streetlights and buildings. Wayne has it down to a science, so that by December everything is ready. The lights stay on until December 26, and continue a few days more if it snows.

In 1973, there was an energy crisis. Teague and his crew had set up everything as usual, but in honor of President Nixon's appeal for energy conservation, the town decided to limit the lights to one tree. McAdenville honored this principle again in 1974. But in 1975, the lights went back on, because people missed them so much.

One thing not many people know about is the Yule Log Parade. In 1950, before the idea for the Christmas lights came up, Bill Pharr suggested a ceremony where the townspeople would put a pine log decorated with ribbons and poinsettias on a red sled and pull it from Pharr Yarns to the gymnasium at the Community Center. This ritual continues today. A brass band leads the parade, carolers sing, and all of the children pull the sled with ropes. I hear they really look forward to having a place on the pull-rope.

At the gymnasium, the yule log is laid in the fireplace, and people drink hot chocolate and coffee and eat doughnuts before a blazing fire. The big moment, of course, is when Santa Claus comes.

The Yule Log Parade makes a wonderful way for the people of McAdenville to come together as a community, as they've always done in good times and bad times. The Christmas lights are for the world to see, but the Yule Log Parade is for the children and the people who live and work in McAdenville.

The nickname 'Christmastown' has become so closely identified with McAdenville that it appears on this entrance marker. Below the marker, a wreath-shaped sign advertises the Christmas lights, which glow from December 1 through December 27. (By Steve Rankin Photography.)

My sister Catherine searched for large nativity statues to create a scene in front of the Baptist church. Over the years, stained-glass windows, white doves, and spotlights have been added to the original stable. The nativity scene is under a dome on a hill covered with sand that has been brought in for the occasion. Chimes of the Baptist church provide Christmas carols. When Wayne Teague finishes his duties, he likes to sit on the curb across from the carolers and unwind. Trying to make that December 1 deadline can be pretty stressful. That crew has been known to be on the job at three o'clock in the morning on November 29 to meet it. The nativity scene remains in place until January 6, the day of Epiphany, which celebrates the coming of the Magi.

McAdenville residents have taken to decorating their porches, yards, and front doors with lights and wreaths. In 1995, there were 375 live trees, and almost 325,000 cars passed through town. Figures for 1997, counting cars and buses, establish that well over a million people came through in each three-week period. People lined up for miles on the interstate.

The mill's office building is a faithful participant in the annual Christmas decorations. (By Steve Rankin Photography.)

One of the many reasons people flock to McAdenville from miles around at Christmastime is to see the lights on the evergreen trees surrounding the lake. Circa 1983. (By Steve Rankin Photography.)

You could say McAdenville's history is written in lights. To rejoice in return of the good days, the town began its annual celebration. Though the lights have become known far and wide, and draw thousands of visitors each year, McAdenville considers them simply a celebration of Christmas.

Stowe-Pharr Mills, Inc., Today

In August 1981, following the loss of my dear friend, Bill Pharr, I was named president of Stowe Mills, Inc. Bill's son-in-law, J. Martin Carstarphen III, known to everyone as "Bip," was named vice chairman, CEO, and treasurer. I retained the title of president until my retirement in 1990. Bip joined the company in 1955 and brings the story of Stowe-Pharr into 1999.

McAdenville's natural beauty catches the eye year-round. But during the Christmas season, as twilight falls, the tree lights command the viewer's full attention. (By Steve Rankin Photography.)

The "McAdenville carolers," outside the Baptist church, seem perpetually in mid-song. (By Steve Rankin Photography.)

Bip Carstarphen:

Legally, the name of our company is Stowe-Pharr Mills, Inc. But in the trade, we're known as Pharr Yarns. The real growth of the company was in the eighties. From about 1978 through the eighties, the company probably doubled in sales. Today, in North Carolina, we're among the top 15 textile companies. Our sales are somewhere around $300,000,000 to $375,000,000. In the early seventies, we had 6,000 employees. Since that time, like all companies, we got more modern equipment and labor-saving machinery. In the Gaston area, we now have around 2,500 employees. Including our plants in South Carolina, Georgia, California, and Europe, we have a total of about 4,000 employees.

McAdenville is one of the last textile towns to maintain a mill village, complete with company houses. In our other locations, we've either torn down the houses or "rehab-ed" them and sold them to employees. At one time, when employees were concentrated in a smaller area, these houses were a good thing. Young people could move in and live there until they got a start. Then they could buy a house or continue renting. Today people drive to work from many locations, and there is less interest in company housing. We still have about 170 in McAdenville, and we will continue to maintain them.

In the greater world, Dan is most noted for establishment of the Daniel Stowe Botanical Garden, bringing a new fame to Belmont. In McAdenville, he has always supported *our goals of preserving the historical buildings and this picturesque setting for future generations. Dan Stowe combines in one man a reverence for the past and vision for the future.*

Works Cited

Miller, Billy Robert. *McAdenville: Spun From the Wilderness.* Original publication: 1982. Third edition: 1987.

Ragan, Robert Allison. *The Pioneer Cotton Mills of Gaston County (N.C.): "The First Thirty" (1848-1904) and Gaston County Textile Pioneers.*

Additional Sources

Blythe, LeGette. *Robert Lee Stowe: Pioneer In Textiles.* Heritage Printers, Inc: Charlotte, N.C. ©1965.

Cope, Robert F., and Wellman, Manly Wade. *County of Gaston.* Gaston County Historical Society: Heritage Printers, Inc: Charlotte, N.C. © 1961.

Ragan, Robert Allison. *Leading Textile Mills of Gaston County (N.C.): From 1904 To the Present and Gaston County Textile Pioneers.*

Stowe, Robert Lee, Sr. *Early History of Belmont and Gaston County, North Carolina.* © 1951. Reprint: 1997. Laney-Smith, Inc.: Charlotte, N.C.

Editor:
Beth Laney Smith

McAdenville is one of the last textile towns to maintain a mill village. Approximately 170 company houses remain in use to this day. The homes feature hardwood floors and distinctive architectural detailing, such as gently arched windows and doorways. The bricks that make up the exterior walls are said to have been made on site by prison labor. (By Steve Rankin Photography.)

J. Martin "Bip" Carstarphen III. (Courtesy of Bip Carstarphen.)

Textile Talk

Bobbin: A spool or reel that holds thread or yarn for spinning, weaving, knitting, sewing, or making lace.

Carding: The process of untangling and partially straightening fibers by passing them between two closely spaced surfaces that are moving at different speeds, and at least one of which is covered with sharp points, thus converting a tangled mass of fibers to a filmy web.

Combing: A process following carding that pulls fibers into more parallel alignment.

Drafting: Attenuating or increasing the length per unit weight of slivers, rovings, etc.

Extrude: To force a spinning-solution through the holes of a spinneret at a controlled rate.

Filament: A fiber of indefinite length.

Loom: A machine for weaving cloth by interlacing warp and weft threads.

Roving: The relatively fine fibrous strands used in the later processes of preparation for spinning. A sliver is drawn out to form a fine rope or roving, which is then spun on the spinning-frame.

Sliver: A thick, untwisted rope of fibers, which is the result of the carding process and is suitable for subsequent processing, i.e. combing.

Spindle: A long, slender stick used in spinning to provide the necessary twist to fibers being formed into a yarn. Spindles may be hand devices or part of a spinning wheel.

Spinneret: A nozzle with holes or slits in it, through which the fiber-forming substance is extruded in the manufacture of man-made fibers.

Spinning: (1) This term is used to cover the process of drafting and twisting fibers in order to produce a yarn. The complete operation of the spinning-frame involves drawing out the roving, inserting the twist, and winding the twisted yarn onto a bobbin. (2) The term is also used to cover the process of extruding a fiber-forming substance through a spinneret, to form filaments. The word spinning is therefore used to cover two distinctly different processes.

Staple fiber: Fibers of a suitable length for conversion into spun yarns.

Synthetic: Produced by synthesis; especially, not of natural origin; man-made.

Twist: The number of turns per unit length of yarn.

Warp: The yarn running lengthwise in a woven fabric.

Weave: The manner of interlacing the warp and weft threads in a woven fabric.

Weft: The yarn running width-wise in a woven fabric.

Worsted yarns: Yarn in which the fibers are reasonably parallel and which is spun from combed wool.

Bibliography:

Collier, Ann M. *A Handbook of Textiles*. 3d ed. Exeter: Wheaton, 1980.

The Heritage Illustrated Dictionary Of the English Language. Vol. 2. Boston: Houghton Mifflin Company, 1979.

Tortora, Phyllis G. *Understanding Textiles*. 3d ed. New York: Macmillan Publishing Company, 1982.

Chapter 5

Getting Away

I will make a palace fit for you and me
Of green days in forests and blue days at sea.

— Robert Louis Stevenson, *Songs of Travel*, XI

The waves of the Atlantic are easily visible from the balcony of my bedroom. (By Ken Hester.)

Opposite: The custom-built gazebo, tucked into a shady cluster of palm trees, provides welcome relief on hot summer afternoons. Both its materials and design echo the architecture of the house.

A Place in the Sun

The first time I went to the beach, I was about ten years old. My parents took the family there on vacation, and after what seemed like a terribly long drive in a car packed with clothes and beach things, we arrived in Wilmington, North Carolina. Our luggage was placed on a streetcar, which the family boarded, and we rode to the Oceanic Hotel in Wrightsville Beach. The Oceanic was a great big, wooden hotel, and its staff served some of the finest meals I've ever had. Waiters were always offering us food from their enormous, loaded trays. For entertainment, everybody went to the Alumina. It was a pavilion by the edge of the ocean, with bowling alleys and other activities. Movies were shown out over the water, on a large screen set on piles.

At high tide, the ocean comes up almost as far as the lawn.

afternoons soaking up the warmth of the sun, gaining what people at that time considered a healthy tan. Now, of course, we know there is risk involved. My dermatologist exclaimed recently, "You sure are giving me good business from being down at the beach for so long!"

During the mid 1950s, I decided to build a vacation house on the coast so that I could spend more time there. I stayed in the old Patricia Hotel in the heart of Myrtle Beach for several months, while my uncle George Stowe and I went around looking at lots. This was not as simple as it may sound. We rode up and down the entire beach, carefully eyeing all the property we passed. Uncle George already had a house down there, so he knew what to look for. He would tell me: "No, don't buy that lot. I've seen water go all the way up to it."

Finally I found an oceanfront lot that appeared to be high enough. It was situated right beside the Chapin house, and it was a beautiful piece of property. The Chapin and Burrough families had been the original developers of Myrtle Beach, so naturally they had had their pick of the most desirably located lots. As it turned out, the piece of land I had my eye on was actually the highest lot in Myrtle Beach. When Hurricane Hazel came through the beach in October 1954, the water rose as high as what would become the front yard. Many of the houses nearby were flooded on the first floor.

Eventually I did get that piece of property, but I still feel kind of bad about the way it happened. A lady in Virginia had bought it from the Chapins in March 1956, and every-one said, "You'll never get that lot, Dan." When she came

But Catherine and I were really itching to try out that surf. I also went fishing at the beach and made my first catch. My daddy was with me, and he bought a bucket and put water in it so that I could carry the fish back home. The fish died before we even made it out of Wilmington, though!

From then on, I always looked forward to our beach trips. My first visit to Myrtle Beach, South Carolina, was in the early 1930s—about the time I was ready to go to Davidson. That area had not yet been built up to the crowded place it is today, with all of its noise and lights. It had a family atmosphere and was still a pretty good place to escape city life.

Back then, people were unaware of the risk of skin cancer from overexposure to the sun, so "lying out" was a popular activity. In my opinion, there was nothing more relaxing. I spent many

My mother (left) and my sister Catherine (right) relaxing near the dunes during a family vacation at Myrtle Beach many years ago.

The house during its final phases of construction.

down for visits, the lady always brought her little dog with her, and it liked to go over to the lot—which was a garden at that time—and take care of its personal business. Even though the odds of buying the land did not look very good, I decided to make an offer. So I spoke to a real estate man, who told me the same thing everyone else had been saying—"You'll never get it." But he approached her with the offer. A little while later, he came huffing and puffing down the beach to where I was and exclaimed in disbelief, "She'll sell it!" It turned out her dog had died.

My beach house was built in 1957. In those days, there was no need to contract the project out. I simply hired a good architect and an excellent superintendent, and we bought the materials and supervised the construction ourselves. The architect was James Cooney of Buffalo, New York. Not only was he a fine architect, but he was also a very capable engineer. Earl Bowen, who would later work on my Seven Oaks house, was the project's superintendent. Together, we made sure the beach house met our own high standards. For example, when I found out the steel foundation requirements for building on that land, I had the builders use double that amount of material. Interior design was done by Julian Morton from Wilmington, who at that time was with Mecklenburg Furniture Company. He arranged the furniture so that upon opening the front door, a person could see all the way through the living room and out to the ocean.

The bricks in the fireplace wall came from a Charleston textile mill that was torn down around the time I built the house. During colonial days, they were used to weigh down ships that sailed over from England to pick up rice grown in the Carolinas.

It can be very windy on the oceanfront at times. After completing construction of the house, we brought in additional trees and shrubs, and planted a dense layer of grass, to help prevent erosion.

Hurricane Hugo plowed through the coast of the Carolinas on September 22, 1989, leaving behind a trail of erosion and debris.

The living room floor is 27 feet above sea level, which is about the same altitude as Conway, South Carolina. So I suppose the house is not likely to be flooded. During Hurricane Hugo, we never even boarded the windows, and the only damage sustained was the loss of some palm trees. I still have insurance on the house, though. I keep thinking I'll cancel it, but then I decide maybe I'd better not!

(left) This photo of my nephew Robert Lee Stowe III was made during the early 1960s. (below) My nephew Harding Stowe, photographed during the same beach trip.

There are five bedrooms in the main house, and each has its own bathroom. The apartment suite has two more bedrooms, which share a bath. For about 25 or 30 years, all of the floors were covered in a wonderfully soft, white carpet. People often commented that because it was white, it would not last—especially with young people visiting the house—but it worked out pretty well. It was finally discarded about five years ago, when a friend of mine named Sally Stowe redecorated the house.

A fireplace makes up one wall of the living room, and that surface continues straight up to become a wall in my bedroom, directly above. The bricks for that wall were manufactured in the 1600s, when North America was inhabited by the English colonies. At that time, rice was grown here for export. Ships were sent over from England to pick up the rice, and in order to add weight for the journey, bricks were put in the holds. When the ships arrived in Charleston, the bricks were removed, and the rice was loaded up and taken back to England. A textile mill was built in Charleston from the bricks that accumulated there. About the time I was planning my house, I found out that the textile mill was being torn down, so I bought enough of its bricks for the fireplace wall. Some were also used in the kitchen brickwork.

The lot was already attractive when I bought it, so there was not much landscaping to be done. Live oak trees had been growing there for years, stunted by the ocean breeze. We did bring in some palm trees. Essentially, we wanted the lot's appearance to remain natural, in keeping with its surroundings.

Even more important to me than any of the ideal aspects of the house was the ability to get away from business yet still have family nearby. My sister, Catherine, and her husband, Bill, liked my house so much that they soon wanted a place of their own. They arranged for the company (Stowe-Pharr Mills) to buy a house two doors down from mine—formerly the Chapins' guest house. Having them so close was wonderful. Bill was not just a brother-in-law to me—he was one of my best friends.

Meanwhile my brother, Robert, and his wife and sons visited the beach and decided they would like a house there as well. Robert had his eye on the house between mine and the Pharrs'. That middle house and the guest house that the Pharrs bought had been built in 1933 and 1934 by Mr. Burroughs and Mr. Chapin. Robert told the lady who owned the place: "My brother built a vacation home on one side of you, and my sister and brother-in-law bought the house on the other side. If you ever decide to sell yours, please let me know, because I would like to have

a house here." The lady called him one day and said she was ready to sell. She asked a reasonable price, and Robert's company (R. L. Stowe Mills) bought the house. Both of the company houses were used by corporate officials and for entertaining business guests.

I couldn't have been more delighted. That day marked the beginning of a whole new era of family get-togethers. The Pharrs, our good friends Caldwell and Jocelyn Ragan, and I hosted occasional parties at the Dunes Club, which were always a hit. But some of the best times we had were spontaneous—those moments when the families happened to congregate at one house or another, and did nothing more than enjoy each other's company. Here I will let my nephew, Harding, share his recollections of the times we all spent down at the beach.

(left) My mother and her sister Florence at my beach house in 1958.

This boardwalk goes from my house onto the beach, allowing easy access in spite of sand dunes and thick plant growth.

Light-colored upholstery and carpet bring the atmosphere of the beach into the living room, while a mirrored wall creates the illusion of more space.

The leafy pattern of the dining room wallpaper calls to mind the palm trees just outside the house. Bright coral, sandy beige, and sea green tones are prevalent throughout the interior.

Harding Stowe:

From about the time I was six or seven years old, my family vacationed at Myrtle Beach. We went for two weeks each summer, and we always coordinated our vacations so that the Pharrs, the Carstarphens, and Dan would be down there at the same time. Dan's house was kind of the place for the grownups—they'd have cocktails over there before dinner. Our house was the kids' hangout, and nobody cared if there were a lot of kids wrecking it or if we had the television turned up too loud.

Still, Dan's place was, in a sense, the center of entertainment. There was a person here in Belmont who had a film service, including a tremendous 16-millimeter film library, and that person rented out movies to theaters all over the country. Before Dan came to the

A game table in one corner of the living room stands ever ready for a spontaneous hand of cards.

beach, he'd rent some of these films, and during a two-week vacation, he'd put on two or three picture shows. We would all have dinner in our own houses and then walk down to his house to watch a movie. Dan loved to get a horror movie that would scare the kids to death! The little ones, like Richmond and Catherine, would be terrified during the whole movie. Dan enjoyed that kind of excitement—the screaming and the hollering. He would also have everybody over for a picnic or for dinner, usually outside. It was a great growing-up experience to have all your family together like that.

Brick walkways run along the side of the house and extend down to the gazebo, protecting bare feet.

Because of the elevation of my property, the ocean is visible over the sand dunes even from the lower level of the house. Architect James Cooney took full advantage of that fact, incorporating a great deal of glass and a spacious porch on the ground floor.

The house itself is interesting. It's a little bit contemporary. I think it was the first house down there that was air-conditioned. For Dan and my father—and for all of my family—air conditioning is a big thing. Nobody had ever heard of having a centrally air-conditioned beach house before.

Another unique aspect of the house was its carpet. DuPont made a very special, ultra-soft carpet back then, and Dan installed it in his beach house. It was amazing, because we had our shoes off so much of the time at the beach, and walking on this carpet felt like walking on fur. And it was all white. Ninety percent of the time, there would be no problem, because it would be Dan and his adult friends and family. But the other ten percent of the time, there were a bunch of kids running around, spilling Cokes and that kind of stuff. Dan never got upset, though.

We just had an awful lot of fun. Dan had a cook named Arthur King, and you could tell that having a bunch of kids around was not Arthur's thing! I think he liked working for Dan, and serving Dan and his guests, but when all these kids would move in, Arthur was a little gruff. He was a good person, though, and he put up with us.

Sunlight streams into the master bedroom from the balcony windows.

The master bedroom's sitting area shares a brick fireplace wall with the living room, situated directly below.

One year, Dan bought all the kids one of those long fishnets on two poles. It would take two people to walk through the water with it, and then we would pull it out to see what we'd caught. And that became a tradition for Dan. He took movies of us fishing with the net for probably ten or 12 consecutive years—and he still has them. He's the type of person who has taken movies and pictures at every event. It's very important to him, if the family is together, to record it on movies and in pictures.

So the beach was a time when the families were together continuously for about two weeks. We vacationed like that in the summer for close to 20 years. My father bought our beach house in 1961, and he had a stroke at the beach in 1979, so we did it for 18 consecutive years—actually longer, because we stayed at Dan's house before we had our own house.

As we got older, Dan continued to invite us to go down to the beach with him. I remember one particular weekend—I was engaged to my future wife, Pam—he had us to his beach house for cocktails with Mr. and Mrs. Pharr. In fact, whenever I let him know we'd be at the beach, he made sure to invite us over. He was very, very good to us.

Impressions are made when you're a child— smells, memories. Walking into his beach house, I still have the same impressions that I remember having at two or three years old. They stay with you. We had a lot of fun at the beach, from the time that I can first remember up until the time that Dan quit going down.

> "It isn't just antiques that need restoration— people do, too."
>
> —Dan Stowe

Alene is after "the big one."

When my father had a stroke, our synchronization of beach trips began to decline. The older generation no longer went as often for various reasons, and the children were now growing up and doing their own things. Traditions change over time.

Like Harding, I miss those vacations we spent together at the beach, but I too realize that things cannot always remain the same. For a long time, I went to Myrtle Beach every weekend, usually heading down on Thursday and coming back on Sunday afternoon. But in recent years, I just haven't been able to get down there. I miss it. For a while, I tried leasing out the house, but I wasn't satisfied with that situation. I would like to always keep the place, though ... as long as I can make ends meet!

My brother Robert sits modestly in the shade of a beach umbrella as I show off my legs!

Heading for the Hills

It's difficult to say which season is the most beautiful here. While it would be hard to beat the magnificence of the leaves changing colors or of winter snows, the spring and summer blossoms sure do give the cooler seasons a run for their money. Barely visible behind the stone wall at the lower left, that gorgeous little speck of white and brown is Alene.

I've already mentioned my impression of the abominable elevator that I encountered during my family's trip to Asheville when I was two years old. Only one part of the trip made a greater impression on me, and that was my first view of the Appalachian Mountains. Kings and Crowder's mountains are not far from Belmont, so I imagine I had already seen a mountain or two by then—but comparing those modest peaks to the expanse and

dizzying altitudes of the Appalachian range is like comparing a couple of picket fences to the Great Wall of China. They just don't stack up.

Later in my childhood, my family took trips to Montreat, which is the Presbyterian retreat near Black Mountain, North Carolina. As a young man, I got more enjoyment from going to the beach, where I could work on my tan. But when I got older and stopped lying out in the sun, I found myself again preferring to vacation in the mountains.

When designing the house, Sherman Pardue kept the elements of its location in mind. The sloping garage roof almost makes the house look like a part of the hill on which it sits. Building into the hillside allowed Sherman to put entrances at both the main and basement levels.

A gently winding staircase, built with stone blocks, leads to the main entrance of the house. Numerous balconies, long windows, and a deck make the most of the scenic mountain view.

When it became time to hire an architect, I couldn't think of a better choice than Sherman Pardue, who had designed the Seven Oaks house. Sherman had also developed a reputation for doing excellent interior design work, so I put him in charge of that as well. My trust paid off. The house he created is marvelous.

Including the basement, it has three stories, with plenty of glass on the exterior to take advantage of the stunning views. The upper level has one bedroom, accompanied by a bath. Its living room is spacious enough that one end functions as a dining room, which opens into the kitchen. On the second level are four bedrooms and an equal number of bathrooms. The basement, primarily used as storage space, is adjoined by a garage. From there, the other two levels may be reached by elevator.

Icicles hanging from the eaves adorn the house with a shimmery touch of winter.

Around 1980, I began to look into buying land on Grandfather Mountain. That location is ideal—it's just off the Blue Ridge Parkway, and it doesn't take very long to get there. Also, some of my family and friends have vacation homes in that area. And I like the altitude. In January 1981, I bought a tract that is just under an acre and a half in size.

A layer of freshly fallen snow turns the front walk into a sledding opportunity that no child could resist.

I always supposed that by the time I reached adulthood, I would no longer have to wear binding snowsuits. Apparently I was wrong.

Approaching the house, the driveway is lined by bright blossoms.

Meanwhile, I finally won over a certain enchanting bathing beauty whom I'd met at Myrtle Beach many years before. Alene and I were introduced by mutual friends in 1972, and it took me 11 years to convince her to marry me. Construction of the mountain house was completed in 1983, just about the time Alene finally declared "she did." We spent our honeymoon there.

I would imagine that most people like to head to the mountains during autumn, when the leaves are showing off their fiery splendor, but Alene and I have enjoyed spending time up there year round. Because of the altitude, the temperature remains pleasantly cool even in July and August. And what could beat passing a wintry afternoon in front of a crackling fire, looking out over snow-dusted slopes and the silhouettes of bare trees?

Carolyn Egeli painted this portrait of me, which hangs over the fireplace mantel.

Never content to sit still for very long, Alene likes to roll up her sleeves and tend to the garden herself. On more than one occasion, I've been afraid she might disappear headfirst into the flowers!

Even during the "off season," there is never a shortage of things to do while we are at the mountain house. Alene has invested a good bit of her time in turning the grounds into something spectacular. She loves to plant flowers, and in the warmer months when everything is in bloom, the beds lining the main walk are a mass of vibrant colors.

I was exposed to travel at an early age, and it has remained a great passion of mine. In 1979, Alene and I took a trip around the world, and visited many of what are considered to be the most interesting and exotic locations on the globe. I've seen the graceful arches and flying buttresses of Notre Dame, the ancient olive trees in the Garden of Gethsemane, and the gorgeous azure waters of Hawaii. I've taken a ship through the Panama Canal. But as it turned out, I never needed to look any further than the Carolinas to find my own two tracts of paradise.

Editors:
Ashley Garner
Beth Laney Smith

Peeking out from the ferns, this fanciful fellow seems ready to dart off through the garden.

Chapter 6

Enriching the Present with Treasures from the Past

"*His preservation of beauty and nature, through the botanical garden and of the various historical properties, is going to make a bigger contribution to the people throughout the region than anything else they've done, individually or collectively.*"

— Robert Ragan;
Gaston County Historian

I have saved many of the things I owned as a child and young adult. I still have the Lionel train I played with in my childhood, and my first camera. In adult life, this onetime hobby grew from gadgets and toys, to architectural components, buildings and houses. And let me not omit—cars. I have stored 12 antique cars, including my mother's 1950 Cadillac. Another item I treasure is a rose stained glass window, which was in the sanctuary of the original First Presbyterian Church here in Belmont. Fortunately I have been able to use my resources and interests to help preserve historical sites and artifacts in Gaston County.

Preservation North Carolina

I have a strong partnership with Preservation North Carolina, and have been involved with the organization for several years regarding many of my endeavors. It is a state program devoted to preserving historic landmarks. Once a person, or an organization like Joint Historic Properties Commission in North Carolina, alerts the group of a possible project, it can provide an avenue for parties to donate money to save buildings and homes from demolition. Therefore, when I contribute to Preservation North Carolina, I do two things: I earmark my contribution to be set aside for a specific cause, and I promote fundraising to supplement the donated sum. I refer to this as a "challenge kind of gift," meaning now that the ball is rolling, it is up to them to see it through.

The John D. McLean House

Probably my most visible adventure in preservation is the McLean House, as it stands near the entrance of my property at Seven Oaks. The estate consists of three separate houses: the main house, an adjacent building once used as a pharmacy, and a storage house.[1] It also includes five or six acres of land called a *vista* around the house. Therefore, the historic designation not only includes the house itself, but also the view surrounding the property. After restoring the main house, I opened a popular antique shop with the help of Mrs. Alice Conner, who ran the store for several years. Eventually, it was closed. Many considered this commercial use unfortunate; however in my eyes, keeping the store open allowed one of the oldest houses in Gaston County to remain standing in good condition, and to be shared with many visitors.

The Lentz Hotel and the Lentz-Springs House

Most recently we have set our sights on the Lentz-Springs house, which was inhabited by the first mayor of Mount Holly, Paul Lentz. In the past, we had relocated the Lentz Hotel in order to save *it* from destruction. Because the house was positioned at the entrance of Mount Holly, a prime location for development, the property was eventually purchased by a large corporation. Either the

The McLean house, also known as the Plantation house. (By Paul G. Beswick, Emeritus AIA, Mableton, GA.)

house had to move, or it was to be destroyed. After working out a plan and organizing funds, the house was bestowed upon Preservation North Carolina, who in turn bought a lot, built a new foundation, and added features like a chimney and front porch. After the renovation, the home was put on the market. Lucy Penegar, a friend and commissioner of the Joint Historic Properties Commission, always laughs, because people refer to the organization as a group that can market "buildings that are either in a bad neighborhood or nobody else can sell them." For the most part, Preservation North Carolina usually has good luck in finding suitable home owners for their properties.

The Lentz-Springs house underwent construction in order to entice future homeowners. (Courtesy of Lucy Penegar.)

The Lentz Hotel, which housed the family and visitors passing through, also served as birthplace and home to Dan's mother, Nellie Rhyne Stowe, whose mother was a Lentz. (Depicted in the artwork of Frans Van Bergen, 1981. By Steve Rankin Photography.)

[1]Please see Chapter 7 regarding the Plantation House.

Now, the Hoffman Hotel serves as the Gaston County Museum of Art & History. (By Steve Rankin Photography.)

The Museum

One of the most interesting projects we undertook was the Gaston County Museum of Art & History in Dallas. The museum, established in 1976, had been confined to the second floor of the old courthouse, built in 1846, to provide a meeting place for the county seat. Just as the museum started to bring in plenty of visitors, the Hoffman Hotel was put on the market. The hotel was located within the Dallas square right in the heart of Gaston County. At the time of the hotel's construction, Gaston County was home to three general stores, churches for every denomination, and a Masonic lodge. In the middle of this bustling town was this beautiful old building. So you can see how the hotel was a perfect location for the museum. The actual value of the hotel was around $100,000, but the owner offered it to the museum for $50,000 with a tax writeoff for that part of the gift. Unfortunately, the bond referendum fell through, which leads to my involvement.

The Joint Historic Properties Commission is affiliated with the museum; however, they work on other projects in Gaston County. They rely on volunteers to save historic sites which are scheduled for demolition or commercial use. The group is directed by seven commission members, which are appointed by county commissioners. Not including external contributions, about $9,000 is distributed to the non-profit organization to fund research, provide leverage for grant money, photography expenses, and many more costs. Lucy Penegar approached me about the project. This is her version of how we saved the museum.

Dan purchased and donated several carriages, then contributed adequate funds to help build a carriage house in which the antique collection is stored.

The Hoffman House Dallas N C

The Hoffman Hotel in the early 1900's. (Courtesy of Lucy Penegar.)

You could tell he was really committed to it from the start. It almost gives me cold chills to think about it. Mr. Stowe started us out with our fund raising, and he gave us our first contribution. When you have your first gift like that, it's easy to go after others. If community members know he's committed and he cares, then they'll be more likely to help, too. We raised about $126,000 in two weeks.

Before the museum moved into the hotel, he and I together found a collection of carriages. It was a nice collection with different styles of carriages and three sleighs. Some of them were like a doctor's buggy, the type that anyone around here would have had. But one of them was called a brougham. It was to be pulled by two horses, and it looks like something Cinderella would ride in.

In 1980, he bought the collection and donated it to the museum. We opened this portion of the museum to the public before the rest was complete. Then Mr. Stowe kept saying, 'You really need a carriage house for those carriages to go in.' So we began to look

This carriage, seen leaving the McLean House, is concurrent with styles represented in the museum exhibit. (By Paul G. Beswick, Emeritus AIA, Mableton, GA.)

We learned that most of the collection was from the Pennsylvania area, and the man who owned the carriages was a Rhyne, an ancestor of my mother's. He purchased the carriages and then brought them to the Gaston County area. So this fact gave me more of an incentive to help, being that the original collector was a relative. Plus, he was very helpful, and insisted on selling the pieces at his purchase cost. He was very generous to the museum and the community.

Dan with Alan Waufle, former curator of the museum, with the new exhibit.

The First Baptist Church

Certainly the most controversial project we addressed was that of the First Baptist Church in downtown Gastonia. Built in 1923 by esteemed Charlotte architect William Rogers, the church was scheduled to be demolished in order to erect an office building. For months preservationists had been haggling with councilmen and trying to compromise with Pearson Properties, who had already made a down payment of $40,000 on the building. In July 1998, as an anonymous party affiliated with Preservation North Carolina, the Daniel Stowe Trust offered a bid of $850,000 to put a stop to the destruction of the 75 year old landmark. Obviously this caused quite a commotion, as the wrecking crew was due to come in just days.

We purchased the property with the condition that it must not be demolished. But we also purchased the property with compromise in mind. We agreed that four acres will be cleared for the office complex, and parking in between the buildings will be shared by the two organizations. It couldn't have been more pleasing to all parties involved. Councilman Walt Mallonee described the contract as a "win-win-win situation." He said, "We [the city of Gastonia] get money back on our investment, economic development with Pearson Properties and we also save a beautiful building."

Saint Stephens A.M.E Zion Church purchased the building in May 1999, with plans to lease part of the space to the Arts Council. The new church, named Unity Place, became a host for several religious ceremonies of all denominations, lectures, theatric performances, and weddings.

Giving Back to the Community

The love for my own personal heritage and southern roots is most easily conveyed by my attempts to preserve historical landmarks in Gaston County. I have plunged into projects wholeheartedly to save what I consider an important tool in teaching future residents, and possible historians, about the generations that founded this area. In short, I wish for everyone to enjoy the beauty and perseverence of buildings, homes, and churches in person, not only in textbooks and memories.

Editor:
Lauren Brisby

The unique and outstanding architectural components prompted the Daniel Stowe Trust to help save the First Baptist Church from demolition. (By Steve Rankin Photography.)

Chapter 7

The Plantation House

"It was not on the way to anywhere."

The historical marker in front of the Plantation House reads: "The John D. McLean House, c. 1848. Plantation home of Dr. John D. McLean (1794-1880), one of first medical doctors in area, following tradition of his father, Dr. William McLean. Ordinance approved June 8, 1989." (By Greg McKee.)

Opposite: On a breezy spring day, the McLean house is the essence of a southern plantation home. (By Paul G. Beswick, Emeritus AIA, Mableton, Ga.)

For most of my life, antiques have fascinated me. My interest in collecting and preserving the craftsmanship of earlier times came largely from my mother, who had excellent taste. My father also appreciated antiques, but he was a businessman with little time for other interests.

During my late teens, I went on trips with my family and sometimes bought a few items. Of course, I was not able to afford much at that time, but I still remember some pieces I wish I had acquired. On one occasion I found the most beautiful inlaid marble table down in Palm Beach. Unfortunately, the price being asked was $400, which was too steep for my budget as a young man.

Even when antiques were beyond my means, the love of fine pieces stayed with me. After I finished college and began work at the mill in McAdenville, I started collecting and storing antiques. Ultimately, this interest and a love of history led me to open the Plantation House.

I obtained the 100-acre tract that included the old McLean house on October 31, 1945. The house had been built by Dr. John D. McLean, and the smaller building nearby had served as his office and pharmacy. No one knows exactly when they were erected, but suggested dates range from 1848 to 1869. Aunt Min recorded in her *History of Gaston County:*[1]

When the house now standing was built, a brick from the old house, bearing the date 1794, was placed in the chimney of the new.

[1]Puett, Minnie Stowe. *History of Gaston County.* © 1939. Reprint: 1998. Laney-Smith, Inc.: Charlotte, N.C.

The exterior of the McLean house before renovation. The most noticeable change was the replacement of this front porch with a two-story, flat-roofed portico. A preservation planner at the State Historical Preservation Office described the house as a "substantial example of mid-nineteenth century Greek Revival architecture." (Courtesy of the Gaston County Historic Properties Commission.)

In 1886, an earthquake moved the McLean house about a quarter of an inch on its foundation. Fortunately, the two big chimneys held the structure together. The side of the house still bears a crack from the movement. My father documented some details of that earthquake in *Early History of Belmont and Gaston County, North Carolina:*[2]

> On August 31, 1886, an earthquake occurred in this country which caused more excitement and fright among the people than anything that had ever happened before. Very few people seemed to realize what it was and a lot of them left home that night and went out to see whether their neighbors' homes shook also, and if they did not, they were not going to stay in their own houses any more. I know a lot of people would not stay at home by themselves for two or three months and some would not sleep in houses. There were more people who got religion just after this earthquake than ever had at any time before, but it did not last and after a few months they got back in the same shape they were before so far as religion was concerned. The earthquake shook the top off a lot of chimneys in this community, but did no real damage to amount to anything. At Charleston, S.C., it did a lot of damage and killed something like 30 or 40 people. There were several quakes the first night, but the first one

[2]Stowe, Robert Lee, Sr. *Early History of Belmont and Gaston County, North Carolina.* © 1951. Reprint: 1997. Laney-Smith, Inc.: Charlotte, N.C.

was the heaviest and did all the damage that was done. For two or three months there would be a quake once in a while, but not a heavy one.

The McLean house was built during the mid-nineteenth-century Greek Revival period. It is made of huge hand-hewn logs, which are squared off and held in place by large wooden pegs. All of its woodwork had been crafted from heart pine, which takes a very long time to deteriorate, so I did not have to do a lot of restoration. Structurally, the building did not need any work, but we removed some of the boards to look inside the walls and check out the construction.

I put a two-story porch with columns on the front of the house, somewhat modifying the appearance of the exterior. However, this did not compromise the historical value of the site. As Lucy Penegar of the Historic Properties Commission once noted: "One does not always take a historic house and restore its original appearance, because doing so might destroy some of the history that happened in the meantime. The porch on the McLean house has become part of the history of the structure." So at the prompting of the Historic Properties Commission, and largely through their efforts, we secured a listing of the McLean house on the Gaston County Historic Properties Register in 1989.

By the time I bought the property, the slave quarters were no longer standing. When I was four or five years old, however, my father and I often drove by the McLean land, and I remember seeing the slave houses then. They were situated one right after another and were beginning to deteriorate at that time. Occasionally I still find big rocks from their chimneys out in the field.

Before long, I began using the McLean house as a storage site. The crops that were raised on my farm took up quite a bit of space, and when my warehouses could hold no more, I had the overflow moved there. The building was soon filled with wheat and oats, and it was so well-built that it was not hurt a bit.

Over the years I began looking for a more meaningful use for the McLean house, in keeping with its heritage. I discussed with my family and friends the idea of running a fine-antiques shop there, and decided that would be the perfect solution.

I was 54 years old when I opened the Plantation House in 1967 and 72 when its doors closed to the public in December 1985. Throughout that time, many fine people kept the shop running. Two of them—Alice Conner, the manager; and Nell Stowe, the business manager—share their recollections in this chapter. They were interviewed separately, and it is interesting to compare their memories of the same scenes and events. I am grateful to Alice for her key role in opening the Plantation House and maintaining it over the years. When she decided to retire in late 1985, I knew it was time to close the shop. She and Nell agreed to stay on until the following May to take care of the remaining details. Today the house is being rented and is once again a dwelling place.

For a year after the business closed, antique lovers continued to stop by and wander into the house. The people who lived there were very nice about it and simply said, "I'm sorry—it's closed up."

Looking back, I would say the Plantation House was a great success. At the time, friends often asked me, "Why in the world do you think people are going to come out here to buy antiques?" I told them, "If you have something people want, they are going to beat a path to your door." And they did.

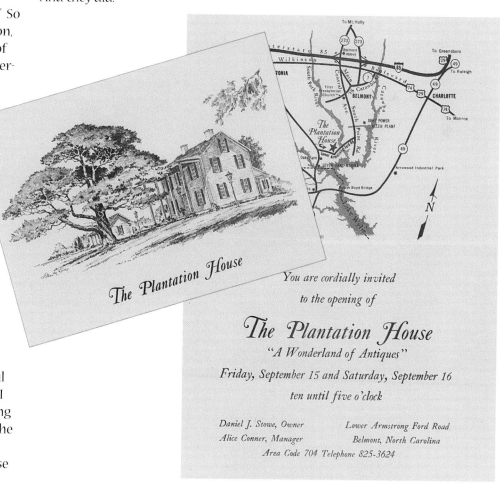

The grand opening invitation. (Courtesy of Mrs. Nell Stowe.)

The Reflections of Alice Conner and Nell Stowe

Opening the Plantation House

"Sally Mason, a friend of mine, recommended me to Dan Stowe," explained Alice Conner. *"She was Catherine Pharr's best buddy, and they were very fond of each other. She told me that Dan wanted to open an antique shop and that she was going to suggest that he interview me. He asked me the next day, and I told him I'd be delighted.*

"In college I majored in English—but I had a natural love of history. My mother and grandmother had taught me a lot about antiques, so I developed an appreciation for these pieces. The history behind the furniture is what makes it interesting to me. I think my favorite period was Chippendale.

"An excellent way to learn about antiques is simply to spend time observing them. After being around authentic antique furniture, you start looking for those traits in other pieces that are supposed to be reproductions.

"The Plantation House opened on September 15, 1967. We had announced it in nearly every local newspaper that we could find, and we served refreshments. It was like a party. I was pleased with the crowd that came, because it was quite a distance from Charlotte—but we always sold to Charlotte people. They could make a morning or an afternoon out of it."

This smaller building was the office and pharmacy of Dr. John McLean. It sits several yards west of the main house. (By Greg McKee.)

"Alice and I were sort of opposites," noted Nell Stowe. *"I'm the organized, nitty-gritty type, and she's the artist. But we got along fine together. I had just met her at the grand opening. I went down one afternoon— took my mother with me, in fact—just to visit. Alice asked, 'Would you be interested in working here?' Our son was in first grade, so I said I could work half a day. She said that would help her a lot, because she would have the*

Blossoming cherry trees line this stretch of my driveway, which extends out to Lower Armstrong Ford Road. The Plantation House, shown here in the background, sits directly across from the end of the driveway. (By Paul G. Beswick, Emeritus AIA, Mableton, Ga.)

mornings free to see clients in Charlotte before driving to Belmont. And then she could be at the shop in the afternoons. So it just evolved, and it was a great relationship.

"I really did not have a background in antiques, so it was a great learning experience for me. I had one related course in college, I think, along with interior design, where you learn the different periods and so forth. So this was wonderful. I had hands-on experience with all these beautiful things. It's a whole vocabulary of its own to learn, too. And I came to know the origins and the names of different things.

"I don't know that I really had a title. When Alice Conner employed me, she said, 'I just need somebody to answer the phone and be here when I'm not here occasionally.' Well, each day new things came in. There was stock to be put away, and there were things to be priced. And then, at the end of the month when it came

time to do the books, she handed those to me. Like topsy, my work just grew, so that I did take care of all the business end of it: inventorying the house at the end of each year with the auditors, and doing all the book work. Alice and I both did everything from polishing the silver and the brass to dusting the furniture.

"Alice is very outgoing, and she was a great salesperson. The antique shop where she had worked had closed, and so she had a following, which was a good beginning for us. She knew the right people from all of her experience in Charlotte.

"Back then we didn't have much competition for fine antiques. There was just the one really nice place in Charlotte, and you know women who like antiques will go to the ends of the earth to find things. It was almost a full day's excursion to come out to the Plantation House. Alice would encourage them by fixing sandwiches and asking them to come for lunch.

"Prices were good back then. They seemed high at the time, but now when we think about the prices of English antiques—why, it was fabulous. And the people—you really meet the most charming people who are interested in that kind of thing. They came particularly through the Southern Accents ad that we had. People traveling would come from states really far away. And the setting was pleasant, too—to come into a house where you really felt like you were on an early plantation and that the owner might have actually brought his antiques over from England."

Eight Rooms Of Treasures

Alice Conner: It was a wonderful, wonderful shop. Dan Stowe liked the best; he wanted the finest of everything. There were eight rooms in that house. We had rooms of furniture, both formal and informal. We had very fine porcelains, lovely crystal, and chandeliers.

Nell Stowe: Upon entering the house, you went into a wide hall, and then there was a parlor on either side, and the dining room behind that. We had what we used as our gift room on the other side. I think that had been a family breakfast room, maybe, when people lived there. The original kitchen had burned, and that had been separate from the house. So the kitchen we had was attached, and that was my office, where we kept fabric samples

and all sorts of things like that. And then you went up the stairway from the front, and there were four bedrooms upstairs.

It was a progressive house in the way it was built, in that there were cupboards beside the fireplace in each room. They didn't have closets back in those days; there were armoires in the rooms. So the building itself was rather progressive for its time. And I used those cupboards to store things for the gift room. There was a fireplace in every room, like I guess all houses had way back then. We never did try to use them, though.

AC: It was a fun shop to work with, because each room could be set up differently. We had a formal English living room, and we had French things in another room.

NS: There was one room of the very early country-type things, and in 1967 when I went to work, that was not the style. We could hardly sell anything out of that room. Everybody wanted the fine English eighteenth-century drawing-room type things. But then

you could really see how styles changed in the United States as the country things became so much more popular, and that became the room where everybody wanted to look. We forget that even antiques go in fads—which style is the most popular at any time. So as people's lifestyles changed to the very informal that we have now, the fad became those early things that perhaps are more crude to us—don't have the fine workmanship that the others did—but are very liveable. That's what I think people now are looking for. We didn't sell French all too often, but that also later came to be far more popular to mix with English than it had been when we first went into business.

In early times before the Plantation House, during wintry days such as this, the fireplaces were put to use. Because fireplaces provided the primary source of heat at the time, one was built in each of the eight rooms in the house. (By Greg McKee.)

The Plantation House
"A Wonderland of Antiques"

"People just loved to have their items wrapped in the Plantation House paper. They thought that made it a special gift!"

AC: And then we had the back room, where people could sit down and eat. We were serving refreshments, so it was fun. The antiques were in the different rooms to carry out the French or the English theme, and to make it more attractive. We had it set up with the proper accessories—such as crystal and china—in each room.

The Gift Boutique

AC: Dan thought it would be wise to have a gift boutique, because some people came in there and didn't want to spend a thousand dollars for an antique, but they still wanted to buy something. So we had a lovely little gift shop downstairs in the second room as you entered, and the rest of the rooms were all filled with antiques. We also had some crystal and china in the gift room, but not antique crystal and china. So the lamps and all of the other antiques were spread around, but the "repros" [reproductions] were in the gift room.

NS: We built up a very good wedding gift business, particularly in Belmont. A lot of people had one particular thing they gave to every bride, and they would call us, and we did big business on the telephone. Brides were even able to register at the Plantation House.

The wedding gifts weren't antiques. They were all new things that brides would like to get. Prices ranged from three dollars to a hundred. I always went with Alice to do the buying for that room, in Atlanta or New York. We tried to find gift items that were a little different—that you wouldn't find in a department store. Everything from distinctive serving pieces and crystal to interesting waste baskets and umbrella stands. Decorative art pieces. Wine glasses and centerpieces. Mantel arrangements. All types of things that we thought were a little different and yet very useful or decorative. People just loved to have their items wrapped in the Plantation House paper. They thought that made it a special gift!

The regular gift shop items came out of the same room. Again, we carried accessories of all types that fit into just about any type of decor, including contemporary and country. These were mostly accessories that people would just like to have as "set-abouts" in their houses. You know how when you take a trip you probably like to bring back a little something that you can set down and always remember, "That's where I got it." That was the type of thing they would buy.

The gift shop's wrapping paper featured a detailed rendering of the Plantation House by artist Gene Love of Charlotte. Packages were wrapped in this unique paper and tied with brown string. (Courtesy of Mrs. Nell Stowe.)

We also made some interesting things. We made lamps out of all sorts of figures and vases and candlesticks. These made very personal and individual pieces for rooms. We did a lot when we were designing a room. We'd find a particular candlestick and we would know a lamp out of that would be just right. It was hard to see some of those things go, but they were sold to people who appreciated them.

Antique-Buying Trips

AC: I had all the joy of buying and selling, looking and finding. Nell did all the work! She knew and kept a record of what we paid for an item and what we received for it and cost of insurance. So Nell did the work, and I had all the fun.

I went to England twice a year to look for antiques. And I went to Scotland to look and to buy if possible, and also to Paris. But England was where I really found what we could sell—what I thought we needed. And then I looked in North Carolina—in Raleigh and the eastern part of the state. I looked in South Carolina. I went down to Charleston and to Atlanta. And then I went up to Richmond and Washington. I looked around. At all these places, I visited the shops to see what they were selling and what they were charging.

Nell usually stayed at the Plantation House while I was away, and she could handle it by herself. When I went to England, I was only gone three or four days. I had already been to England many times beforehand, so that was easy.

NS: I was able to go along with Alice sometimes to buy. I went to England one time with her. We had contacts over there—some were up in Norwich and in London. We would go to the flea market end of London, as well as to very fine dealers. We never knew where we were going to find some goodies. So there were dealers that we dealt with every year. We knew what their things were. And we would get on the tube and just go all over to find these wonderful little places to shop. A lot of them would be in the scrappiest looking areas of London, and in these old ramshackle buildings. I remember thinking, "Where are we?" But we'd open the door and go in, and here were just treasures. It really was exciting. We would spend about five days, and we worked all day every day, going first in one direction and then in another to buy from these people.

And then the antiques were shipped over here by Sealand in big containers. It was always fun the day they arrived and were unlocked, and we began to uncrate each thing and see what we had bought. It was just like Christmas in July. We usually got about two shipments a year, so while we were on buying trips we really worked.

Of course, we didn't do all the buying overseas, because we needed to replace more often than we could go over there. So we would purchase antiques from estate sales in our own country. These sales were mostly in the East. One doesn't find as many things in the West, because it was populated so much later. Sometimes I accompanied Alice on those trips, but usually I kept the shop while she was gone.

Antique Shows

AC: And we did shows. We had a space at the Salisbury Antique Show, because Salisbury is very oriented for antiques. We did one in western North Carolina—Asheville. The best show was the one in Charlotte, because it was the biggest. It was a lot of work to transport all these antiques and set up the displays. But it paid off. We got the publicity, and we made the sales.

Others Who Helped Make It Happen

AC: Mr. J. B. Holcomb and Mr. James Ragan, two men employed by Mr. Stowe on his farm, used their trucks to move the furniture that we sold at the shows.

NS: The fine men who worked on Mr. Stowe's farm also delivered the items that we sold at the Plantation House. Mr. Eb Phillips and Mr. Holcomb were two of those men, and they were both very helpful and courteous. They lifted heavy furniture for us, too. It takes some strong backs to run a business like that, and if you can't deliver on time and with care, then your business can get into deep trouble. So I consider those men a really important part of the business. I'm sure they got very put out with us, because we were always rearranging the rooms. Bless their hearts! They were very patient with moving furniture, upstairs and down. And then moving it again—and again.

AC: Mary Chamberlain assisted at the shop, too—she lives in Charlotte.

NS: At different times there were different young women who would come out about one day a week to give Alice a little more time off and to make sure that we weren't left there alone. Of course, back then we didn't think a thing about being in the building alone all the time! Now we might not feel quite as good about that.

Later on we had a very fine designer there—Dorothy White. She was such a creative lady, whether it was with fabrics, furniture, food, flowers—whatever. And in that way we did a lot more with upholstered furniture and with draperies—complete room design in people's homes, instead of just selling them a piece of furniture. She was a great addition to the staff and was there about three years.

Architectural Details

The stairs are located in the central hall, leading from the main entrance to the second floor. The graceful curve of the stair brackets, shown here, is the only decorative element of the staircase. (Courtesy of the Gaston County Historic Properties Commission.)

The front door lock, viewed from the interior of the house. (Courtesy of the Gaston County Historic Properties Commission.)

The depth created by the chimneys was put to use for built-in cabinets such as this one. The cabinets extend down to the ten-inch baseboard, which continues around the room. (Courtesy of the Gaston County Historic Properties Commission.)

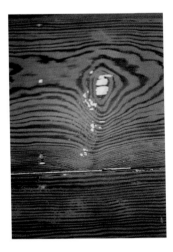

Windows in the main part of the house are the sash type, six-over-six. The area surrounding each of them features minimal molding and simple sills. (Courtesy of the Gaston County Historic Properties Commission.)

Flooring throughout the main part of the house was crafted of heart pine planks of varying widths. (Courtesy of the Gaston County Historic Properties Commission.)

The central front doors are framed with sidelights and a transom. Each sidelight is decoratively composed of three triangular sections. A matching door, without the transom and sidelights, is located at the other end of the central hall on the first floor. (Courtesy of the Gaston County Historic Properties Commission.)

The History of the McLean House

NS: *The house was interesting to people who came, because they wanted to learn about Dr. John McLean, who had built it, and how Sherman had come through, and the slave quarters.*

The house was not burned by Sherman's men—I think the chickens were taken and so forth, but they didn't destroy the house. I was told that the McLeans' youngest son was hidden in the cane break to keep Sherman from conscripting him into the army as he came through. I always thought that was a good story. It was told to us by the descendant of a slave. He said that

The fireplace in each of the eight rooms is simple yet elegant in design. Most of the mantelpieces are decorated only by a gracefully curving entablature. Two of the mantels are distinguished by slightly more complex patterns. The mantel is supported by pilasters which have been scribed with two straight lines, in some cases, or left plain. Hearths are beveled slabs of stone. (Courtesy of the Gaston County Historic Properties Commission.)

his father, or somebody, is the one who hid him. Also, Sam Houston is supposed to have come that way at some point. We had to have a good understanding of the history of the place in order to answer all of the questions that people asked.

There were people still living here while the shop was open who remembered going to the house in the early days when the McLeans were there. They would have a hoe-down—with fiddlers—and a great dance. And so these people would come to the Plantation House and talk about the days they remembered. Zada Rankin, who later married a Stowe, had rented a room

there while she was teaching in a one-room schoolhouse on New Hope Road. She said, "My one memory of this house is being cold!" And it was cold. It's on the hill, and the ceilings are high, and it's not insulated like homes today. And it has those tall windows. So it was very cold in the winter. We had a furnace upstairs and one downstairs, too. Dan used to sometimes send us homemade soup and cornbread to eat with it. That was always a nice surprise on a cold winter day! The place really never did get overly heated.

Festivities and Entertaining

NS: *On occasion, we had special events at the Plantation House. We decided that when the trees along the driveway were in bloom, we would have a Cherry Blossom Luncheon. Alice was in an automobile accident a couple of years before we closed, so she was not at the shop at that time, but Dorothy White and I were still there. We sent out invitations to all of our really good customers in Statesville and Charlotte and everywhere. I guess close to a hundred women came that day. They loved seeing those pretty cherry trees, and we had a nice box lunch. So that was a really fun day.*

At the end of the first year, we had an anniversary party, and then the year that Dan's house was on the Mint Museum tour of homes we included the Plantation House. That took place in the fall, and we had cider so that when the visitors came in the door they could smell the hot cider, and that fit in with long ago, too. We felt like the Plantation House was part of the draw when people came out to tour Dan's house. It was also good advertising for us, because a lot of people came who wouldn't have come just to see the shop.

Sometimes book clubs or garden clubs would ask to come, and one of us would give a little lecture on antiques. Book clubs mainly came. We'd give them a tour of the house, and we would serve refreshments. When there was a tour of homes in Gastonia, sometimes the Plantation House was included, and we would serve refreshments for that. That was another way of getting people in. I especially enjoyed having clubs come there and giving lectures for them. I was able to tell them about the origin of a lot of things and how they got their names and so forth.

Special Items and Their Storage

NS: *At one time we had the brass fittings from the bank of Stanley—the little town just north of here. I believe we sold those to the University of Alabama. A lady came up here, and she drove a Ryder truck home with all those fittings in it—the brass cages that the tellers stood behind, and the marble counter tops. It was quite a layout, and it easily filled a room. And she drove that back to Tuscaloosa, Alabama, where the architecture students at the university were going to help reassemble it and put it in the museum there, to show an old-timey bank. So that was an interesting thing to have, and I would love to see it set up again.*

We stored a few things such as that bank in what had once been the turkey house. That was where our extras stayed. But we kept most things in the main house, because change of temperature is hard on furniture. Cracks might sometimes develop, especially in older pieces.

Closing the Shop

NS: *If the Botanical Garden and the nearby housing developments had been there at the time, it would have been great. But we really were not on the way to anywhere. So it meant one made a special trip when coming to the Plantation House. It took about a half a day by the time one came and went.*

AC: *The Plantation House closed in May 1986. We announced the closing several weeks before we did close and sold everything at a reduced price. Christie's of New York came and bought the whole works, so the closing was sad—I was sad. But 11 years is a nice length of time, and I'm an old lady. I loved working at the Plantation House—it was a wonderful, wonderful experience. I enjoyed every minute of it.*

NS: *After the last of the antiques was hauled away, Dan had the house renovated. He did the most fabulous job of making a modern kitchen and bathroom in it. Those were the things that had made me think, "How in the world will he make it liveable for today?" But he did a fantastic job, and I think the same people have lived there ever since the Plantation House moved out. They wanted an older home, and so it's nice to have somebody who appreciates history living there.*

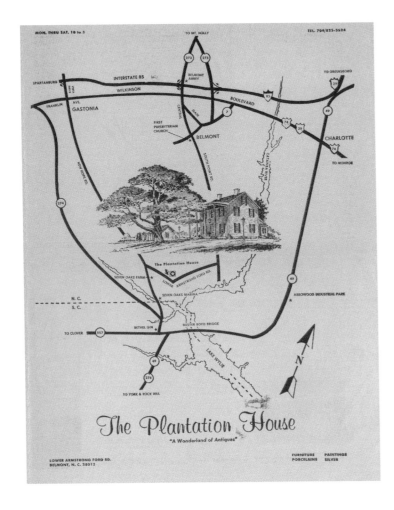

Some of the visitors arrived at our open house festivities by boat, while others came by car. A red-fringed black surrey met the guests at the Seven Oaks marina and escorted them in old-fashioned style to the Plantation House. (By Paul G. Beswick, Emeritus AIA, Mableton, Ga.)

I think this has been a very special love of Dan's life. He was reared with antiques, and he's always appreciated them so much that sometimes I think the Plantation House may have brought him the most happiness of anything he has ever been involved in. And he still talks about how he wishes he had some of that back!

To this day, people tell me, "I miss the Plantation House and the service that I got." I think that is a wonderful compliment.

*Editor:
Ashley Garner*

Chapter 8

At Home on the South Fork

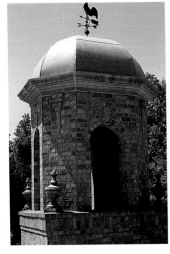

This tower, a part of the addition to the original house, is clearly visible from the river and serves as a distinctive landmark for passers-by. (By Rick Haithcox Photography.)

I t was like the refrain of a love song that lingers at the edge of your thoughts. I speak of the Seven Oaks farm, and most specifically the hillside that overlooks the South Fork. In October 1945, before I even finished my naval service, I bought the tract of 100 acres that had been owned by Dr. John McLean. I built a weekend retreat here in 1947, and came to know the lay of the land and every cove of the waterfront. After it burned down in 1963, I began planning a much larger, permanent residence in its place.

Opposite: Seven Oaks is situated on a hillside overlooking the confluence of the South Fork and Catawba rivers. I think the architect did an excellent job designing a house that blends in with its natural surroundings. I chose an old type of Charleston brick that was discontinued shortly after I bought the materials for the original house. Fortunately, I purchased more bricks than were needed, and the remainders were used in constructing the annex 25 years later. (By Rick Haithcox Photography.)

The building of Seven Oaks has been fulfilling in several ways, to many people—including the architect, the builder, the designer, and numerous craftsmen. I hope it has also fulfilled the location's potential. This site is ideal for a dwelling place—beside river waters, yet high enough to give an exhilarating view. Even the terrain was cooperative, yielding a source of abundant, pure water after we had drilled through 600 feet of granite. The well that was established now generously provides 50 gallons of water a minute.

Seven Oaks has been my finest opportunity to express my concept of the continuity of life. I have been able to make use of components that I'd been storing in a warehouse and give them a new capacity, a new spirit. There is deep satisfaction in knowing that timbers from the first Chronicle Mill building, planed from heart pine, are now a part of my kitchen. The Chronicle Mill foundation also provided bricks for the floor and the fireplace wall. Doors that once served a seventeenth-century house near Windsor Castle in London have become an entryway from the terrace at Seven Oaks. While browsing around an antique store in New Orleans, I came upon the fireplace accessories. Stained glass windows that once intensified reverence in the old First Presbyterian Church in Belmont, built in 1913, now enrich the atmosphere of the annex. And my very favorite acquisition was the Tiffany glass chanced upon in a New York warehouse and now highlighting the library bar with its amber glow, its whimsicality.

This stained glass window came right out of First Presbyterian Church in Belmont. They tore that church down, and I hated to see them do it, but I did get two windows. My parents, Aunt Min's family, and I attended church there for many years. (By Rick Haithcox Photography.)

The stained glass in the library bar was in the warehouse of an antique shop in New York City. They didn't know what to do with it. And I didn't either, at the time! I bought it for a pretty good price. All of that is Tiffany glass. The molding around it is hand-carved, and those three circles in the center represent the Trinity. (By Rick Haithcox Photography.)

Sometimes this recycling comes about in an unexpected way. For instance, the bar in our swimming pool area was constructed from a walnut tree that grew on my farm. When Hurricane Hugo brought it down, I had it rough-hewn and stored. After we began the annex, I sent the wood to a cabinet-maker in High Point, who crafted and finished the units. I like to say I'm the only man I know who *grew* his bar.

Why French design in South Point?

Often I am asked: "Why a house of eighteenth-century French design in South Point?" This decision grew out of my travels in Europe. I would take pictures of buildings and houses I liked, and save them. When Sherman Pardue and I began work on this project, he welcomed this design direction. He was able to establish the ambiance of ancient France and give it new vitality with contemporary innovations. For instance, I wanted a *bow* window in the living room, in contrast to the usual bay window. A bow window is a rounded bay window, with the same projection from the wall. Sherman accommodated my wish with his usual finesse. When I requested a sunroom, he resisted, saying "no one uses them anymore." But after it was built he declared it his favorite room in the house.

Traveling along one of the walkways, you will encounter a whimsical compass design in the midst of the routine pavement. I had a surveyor come out here to establish the precise points of the compass before the stonecutter crafted and laid this piece. (By Rick Haithcox Photography.)

Another specific request I asked of him was for many arches. I had seen the recurring arches at Pompeii in Italy and was enchanted by their grace. Sherman found ingenious ways to use this form, creating a kind of architectural poetry.

Seven Oaks has captured the imagination of many others who have written of it with more descriptive words than I command. The Auxiliary of the Mint Museum of Charlotte featured it in their 1973 Home and Garden Tour, and this description appeared in their brochure:

Seven Oaks is not so much a house as it is an experience, a joint undertaking by the owner, architect and builder. It was begun without a plan but rather with a purpose—to make that lovely site habitable—and for the house to become simply part of the hill. A house of many moods—it has borrowed much from the world—a chandelier from an Indian palace, a table from an English estate, a marble mantel from a chateau outside Paris.

The brickyard manufactured pieces specifically for these concave arches outside the solarium. Custom-made brick was also used for the curved detailing around the dining room windows. (By Paul G. Beswick, Emeritus AIA, Mableton, Ga.)

I had a weekend-type house on the hillside, and it burned. The chimney was the only thing that was left standing, and I didn't want to tear it down. So we built a greenhouse, which we call the conservatory, around that chimney. (By Rick Haithcox Photography.)

95

I got those gates from England. As I understand, they were the property of a house built in 1772 at Hampstead Heath, and they're hand wrought. I believe they were bought for an executive of the Dutch East India Company or one of the big companies that it did business with. After the owner passed away, the house was used as a convent for girls. A friend of mine who lives in England called me one day and said, "They're tearing down this old building, and they've got these beautiful gates, and I want you to have them." He had the pillars knocked down, but he put a lot of dirt out there so that when the capitals fell they didn't break. I had Sherman Pardue design square, brick columns to fit those capitals, and he spaced them to fit the ironwork of the gates. (By Paul G. Beswick, Emeritus AIA, Mableton, Ga.)

I got a pair of these large, antique copper lamps from Edinburgh, Scotland. They are hung on the exterior of the house, at either side of the living room window. The mountings for the lamps are made of hammered bronze. (By Rick Haithcox Photography.)

Diverse Talents Bring Substance to a Dream

Earl Bowen, master builder, was a part of the design scene from its beginning. I had known and worked with him before and developed great respect for his capability and honesty. We agreed before construction began that he would take on no other projects until the Seven Oaks house was built.

Sherman Pardue and I had met at a party in Myrtle Beach. Thereafter I visited houses he had designed in Charlotte and felt he would understand my point of view. He did.

There was another creative giant who brought a magnificent sense of style to the final interiors—William C. Pahlmann, FASID (Fellow, American Society of Interior Designers). I had seen his work featured in magazines and knew of his fame. But what really moved me to engage him was seeing in detail his interior design of the house and yacht of a friend in Boston.

Alice Conner of Plantation House fame searched the United States and abroad for treasures to enrich the interiors, to make them relaxing and comfortable.

Construction began in 1968 and took three and one-half years.

Remembering the Beginning

Sherman Pardue is a philosopher and poet, in addition to being an architect of great skill. Here he shares his memories of the adventure of Seven Oaks, from the early days of studying the terrain:

We stood in the far corner of the polo field with our binoculars by the river. Our sherpas and our runners moved up the rise and into the trees, holding aloft long bamboo poles to which large flags had been attached to mark the extremities of the house. And we, from that great distance, directed their movements until finally we had placed the house part way up the hill. We were creating what in olden times would have been called a 'baronial seat.'

Pahlmann came, and we had lunch and sat upon the lawn and voiced to each other our great expectations until finally we were confident of ourselves and each other— enough so to know that we shared the same vision of the house-to-be.

From *Directory of the Ancestral Heads of New England Families,* **by** Holms:

*"Stowe, Stow—
a fixed place or
mansion;
a town or
garrison..."*

Wearn Lumber Company did most of the millwork in the entire house. As you can see, they did a great job—it's very clear cut. My portrait was painted by Joe King from Winston-Salem, who is most noted for having done a painting of Queen Elizabeth. The lacquered coffee table was custom designed from the paneling of an eighteenth-century Chinese bed. (By Rick Haithcox Photography.)

Wildlife has always taken refuge at the Seven Oaks location. Much of it was driven down from Belmont and New Hope Road by activities of settlers. Our inherited population included foxes, raccoons, and deer. I added peacocks and bantam chickens when I built the weekend retreat. The peacocks and their kith and ken have shown no resentment at this greater intrusion, and strut about as though Seven Oaks is their home too. There have been times when they made themselves too much at home. Alene still comments about discovering some strange deposits on the logs in the living room fireplace. They proved to be peacock droppings. These regal creatures had decided to roost upon the chimney—with this inevitable outcome. We hastily found a way to correct this habit, installing a chimney cap that has to be removed when a fire is lighted.

Other fowl have been more traditional in their ways. Recently a visitor stopped talking mid-sentence when she heard a rooster crowing outside the library. I had to explain that many roam the grounds, along with their families, and I love their company. In fact, I wouldn't be happy in life if I couldn't hear roosters crowing through-out the day. You might say I'm a chicken person. When I was 14, I had four to 500 baby chicks in the rear of our Main Street house.

Sherman here speaks of the wildlife company we enjoyed during our planning stage, and of the excitement we felt as we watched the walls come out of the ground:

Peacocks preened and foxes watched while noisy squads of guinea hen moved in quickly to keep order. The sound of hammering rose up and echoed in the forest and floated away each evening on the passing river, only to be renewed again next morning as we built.

Each morning, we were buoyed on a wave of great excitement and walked the tops of newly-laid walls as the house rose brick on brick out of the ground. These were heady times.

The unflappable Mr. Bowen, Dan and I were a triumvirate—rulers of a remote principality of building materials stacked beneath the tall trees. We laid out our ideas directly upon the ground and moved about with a properly serious and critical eye, making changes as we went.

A copper urn and thick shrubbery frame this corner, but what really draws the eye here is the antique doorway. I bought these doors in 1961. They were originally part of a house near Windsor Castle in London, and they are several hundred years old. (By Rick Haithcox Photography.)

Selecting Brick and Roof Material

In choosing brick for the house, I wanted to avoid the lusty red that is often used in our Piedmont. I found gentler hues—peach and bisque tones—in a brick manu-factured in Charleston. Fortunately, I bought more than needed so that when we built the annex, I had an available supply. This brick is no longer being manufactured. For construction, I had two of the finest masons in the country, one of them living in Belmont. I like to go outside and just look at the patterns they created. They made brick-laying an art form.

"In all it was three years, and when it neared completion there was time for great smiles and good cheer all around at our accomplishment. The closeness you feel with someone when you share a dream is the same kind of feeling you have when you do physical labor with somebody."

—Sherman Pardue

When we discussed the roof material, Sherman said: "Well, I think maybe terne metal would be good. It's a simple material. Some of the houses of parliament have terne metal roofs on them. It's an old English roofing material—goes back to Cornwall and the tin mines, which were actually discovered by the Roman Legions when they occupied Britain." I think the roof fits the spirit of the house, and I have not regretted this choice. We painted it the green of weathered copper, which is a good companion to the brick's warmth.

A Man's House

Pahlmann had focused his talent upon making this a *man's* house, reflecting a *man's* character. I was single at the time, so it was an appropriate and appreciated environment. Seven Oaks quickly projected a feeling of stability and permanence. The floor is stone in the entrance hall, and wood, brick, or tile in the remaining rooms. The walls are plastered—only the dining room has wallpaper. My bedroom has panels of stretched fabric, a provision of Mr. Pahlmann allowing me to change the material for a totally new look. Actually, I haven't changed the fabric in all these years. We came upon a swatch in the attic recently, and it looked exactly like that on the walls.

The plastering technique was developed by Sherman himself. He sought out a plasterer who would follow his direction precisely, and this one workman did all the walls. Sherman didn't want them to reflect two different styles. Here he speaks of this process:

Close-up of the unique wall texture, as described by Sherman Pardue. (By Rick Haithcox Photography.)

I actually went into a closet and did the first plastering myself. I didn't want him to do anything with a trowel which would show a mechanical pattern. I didn't want waves or anything like that—I just wanted clouds. When the stuff we flicked on the plaster was nearly dry, we took the trowel and put a sheen on it, which changed its color. And then we rubbed the whole thing down with a burlap bag, and this gave it its soft edges—no sharp fingers sticking out or anything like that. It's a very unusual treatment, but in rooms that go up 23 feet in height, it's a very effective way to lend some weight to the walls so they don't just sort of drift out of the room.

"The physician can bury his mistakes, but the architect can only advise his client to plant vines."

— Frank Lloyd Wright

Seven Oaks was greatly influenced by the houses I saw during my travels in Europe. Here we see the front facade of the house. The mansard roof is terne metal, and the brickwork is Flemish-bond. (By Paul G. Beswick, Emeritus AIA, Mableton, Ga.)

The dining room table and Hepplewhite chairs were my mother's. That alcove commands a beautiful view of the river and grounds. It is set off from the dining room by three arches, which are a recurring theme in the house. (By Paul G. Beswick, Emeritus AIA, Mableton, Ga.)

Also a House for My Mother's Antiques

This had to be even more than a *man's* house—there were my mother's antiques to consider. So when you enter the dining room at Seven Oaks, you are suddenly in the ambiance of a lady of taste. Her table, chairs, and sideboard establish elegance and rich memories.

The room would be unremarkable architecturally, even with its generous dimensions. But then its expanse terminates with the alcove, a space surrounded with windows that overlook the gardens. You can sit at the dining room table and enjoy the view outside—but you keep wanting to go lean against a wall in the alcove and enjoy your dessert.

Within the alcove is a lighting fixture from my mother's dining room. I was four years old when I first walked into the new house on North Main Street, and that fixture caught my eye. It has real butterflies pressed between two layers of glass, and they haven't deteriorated through all these years.

My most prized antique in the dining room is my highchair—and I can remember sitting in it.

Mother's furniture and paintings also bring the grace of long ago to the living room and library. I think she would like the home I have given them.

We planned the landscaping immediately around the house to pose a striking contrast to the surrounding woodlands. I have always enjoyed the beauty of the land in its natural state, so we tried to disturb that as little as possible. We brought in a wide variety of plants, and some of them are at their peak at any given time of year, so the colors around here are always changing. This scene was photographed from the tower, but one would have to be daring to climb up there for the view! (By Rick Haithcox Photography.)

We enjoy trimming the main entrance of our home for Christmas each year. Sometimes, though, the most beautiful touch is added by our Creator. The scene captured here just wasn't complete until snow flurries caught us by surprise, dusting the grounds with seasonal white. (By Greg McKee.)

The birdbath in front of the conservatory is surrounded by a multitude of flowering plants, creating a small, inviting garden.

The conservatory is situated between the main house and a towering white oak tree. The three rounded arches at the doorway recall similar detailing at the entrance of my house. Because of the dense growth of trees surrounding it, the conservatory gets only enough light for growing ferns. (By Rick Haithcox Photography.)

This is the foyer, as captured by photographer Paul Beswick in 1981. A man from Connecticut did the custom ironwork for the stairway. Each section of the railing has seven acorns and seven oak leaves. (By Paul G. Beswick, Emeritus AIA, Mableton, Ga.)

Wearn Lumber Company crafted all of this paneling and these three doorways, which open into the sunroom. The arch motif, which is prominent on the exterior of the house, is carried inside by the design of these doors. (By Rick Haithcox Photography.)

The Foyer

The foyer at Seven Oaks is functional, yet undeniably impressive. There are curved stairways on either side, the balustrades featuring ironwork with a design motif of oak leaves and acorns. I looked everywhere to find a craftsman for these railings and even had a set made in this part of the country—but they didn't look right. Then I found a blacksmith in Connecticut, who came down and saw what I wanted. He designed it, putting seven oak leaves and seven acorns in each panel. And he beat every bit of that out by hand. He was temperamental. Sometimes I would find a piece of railing flung out in the courtyard, but he would always simmer down and bring it back.

The same workman designed a plaque with my initials, which hangs on the wall opposite the main entrance. I hadn't asked him to do this, so I value it highly. At the top of the plaque are two swords, which actually can be pulled out.

The stairways lead past windows with recessed wooden panels that fold during the day to admit light. One of the stairways winds down to the basement recreation room.

The antique Oushak rug continues the warm apricot and orange tones that begin with the exterior brick. Detailing and atmosphere of the foyer are previews of rooms that are both grand and welcoming.

The Library

To the left of the foyer is my library, a space of both rich architectural detailing and pure fun. You can't find the world grim when you survey the recessed bar and its golden lighting. The room is an inviting retreat with comfortable seating and large windows, from which you can see the families of bantam chickens clucking about. Three arched doors open into the solarium, or sunroom, and give still closer union with nature and her moods.

(By Paul G. Beswick, Emeritus AIA, Mableton, Ga.)

The Living Room

The foyer leads straight ahead into the living room, somewhat vast, measuring 35 feet by 22 feet, and with a 23-foot ceiling. This large room was a first requirement for Seven Oaks, because I love to share its grandeur. We have parties with 50 or more people, and they fit comfortably in this space. The area can become a theater, with a screen that drops down over the entrance to the library.

There are several small rooms that provide storage for office and film-projection equipment. The living room leads into the dining room, adjacent to the kitchen.

The living room ceiling is 23 feet high. There are three balconies overlooking the living room, including this one from my bedroom. (By Rick Haithcox Photography.)

(By Paul G. Beswick, Emeritus AIA, Mableton, Ga.)

The bow window in the living room allows a magnificent view of the waters where the South Fork and the Catawba merge. The rivers join right up above our land. (By Rick Haithcox Photography.)

Plans for the living room fireplace were drawn up by Sherman Pardue. There's a place in Charlotte that did all kinds of stone work for me, and they chiseled the fireplace and mantel out of a big limestone block. The idea of the grapevine motif was taken from a vineyard near the house. For the fireplace wall, we couldn't find stones of this size and color locally, so I believe we got them up around North Wilkesboro. I found the andirons in New Orleans, and they're very old. I also found the altar rail in New Orleans and added the glove-leather padded top. The coal bucket was hand-hammered, and it won first prize at a fair in Europe in 1865. The ornaments on the mantel are eighteenth-century Chinese cloisonne pieces. The bronze and crystal chandelier is made of a pair of fixtures from a maharajah's palace in India. It is attached to an electric hoist, so that at the press of a button it can be lowered to the floor for more convenient cleaning.

(Large photo: By Paul G. Beswick, Emeritus AIA, Mableton, Ga. Inset: By Rick Haithcox Photography.)

The beams and fireplace mantel in the kitchen are solid heart pine. They were taken from the Chronicle Mill, which was the first cotton mill my daddy opened. (By Paul G. Beswick, Emeritus AIA, Mableton, Ga.)

The Kitchen

Very often men say the kitchen is their favorite room in my house. It is inviting with its huge fireplace, heavy beams, and worn brick floors. But it is also a very functional space. There are both gas and electric stoves, and a commercial refrigerator with several doors. One of four freezers is located in the kitchen, and the others are scattered about in different parts of the house. The vegetable gardens of Seven Oaks are productive, so we use all this freezer capacity. We can prepare and serve dinner for at least 12 people from this kitchen—at which times we make good use of two dishwashers.

Personal Space

Upstairs there are three bedrooms and adjacent baths. A suite that was designed for the housekeeper has now become my office and has almost disappeared behind all my stored items. The recreation room in the basement appropriately has peacock-patterned wallpaper and one of the earliest phonographs in the nation, which actually still performs. This is a favorite space for children in the family.

And Then the Annex

The rooms in my house are large and numerous, but I am a collector. Alene and I married in 1983 and her only complaint about Seven Oaks was that it hadn't enough closets. I teased her by saying: "Yes, if you were designing a house, you would want more closets than living or sleeping space." I was feeling the need for a *different* kind of space. My collections of photographs and 16-millimeter film and other family memorabilia needed their own storage. My library was designed with this in mind, but it had reached "standing room only" years ago. So, in 1993 I called Sherman Pardue for another meeting. I asked him to design an annex that would appear to have been here from the beginning. When I review the result from any angle, I think he succeeded brilliantly. In fact, the house has become even more an adventure in its blending of contemporary and French themes.

We converted the former garage into a media room, where a huge screen drops down for television or film viewing. The room is large and equipped with surround-sound. Even with its humble beginning, the wide window gives an expansive view of the courtyard, the woodland, and the families of gamecocks. Comfort is the keynote here—comfort in a working environment, for Alene uses the conference table to sort out her mail-order catalogs, competing with my photo collections. Her computer, color printer, and film-editing equipment are also set up here.

This is my bedroom, largely unchanged from the time the house was built. It remains a favorite haven. (By Paul G. Beswick, Emeritus AIA, Mableton, Ga.)

Adjacent to this is the swimming pool area, which, with its lofty expanse, is easily the most dramatic space at Seven Oaks. The annex includes two shower rooms and a two-story garage with a guest suite above it. Because of sloping of the terrain, we were able to construct the two-story garage with entries from the north and south.

Sherman capped the house with a tower that suggests a lookout from ancient days, an inspired finishing touch. It all reached conclusion in 1995.

The final Seven Oaks house comprises 16,000 square feet—10,000 in the original and 6,000 in the annex. But these are physical dimensions. The final Seven Oaks house is a refuge that indulges every mood. It provides a view of sunrise over the water with morning coffee. Throughout the day its many windows let you feel a part of the life outside—life rich with sound and color and growth. And when day ends, these rooms welcome friends and family for sunset fellowship—or encourage you to relax and close the world away. One feels these are enchanted spaces that allow you to discover new dimensions of yourself.

I was pleased with the way Sherman Pardue used dramatic angles, variations in structural height, and wide expanses of glass and brick to make even the rear of the house appealing. From this side, some of the highlights of the annex can be seen: the swimming pool area to the right, the entrance to the two-story garage, and the tower. (By Rick Haithcox Photography.)

This sprawling boat house greets visitors who come in by the river. It has been the scene for many water-oriented parties, as well as board meetings of the Daniel Stowe Botanical Garden.

The room of the pool. The most difficult and expensive thing was that top window—the skylight. I didn't want the pool too deep, because it's really for exercise. And we've got jets in there. When you turn them on, you can't walk into the water without almost being pushed back. I've been in the pool when there was snow on the ground. It's sort of fun to be in a pool and looking out on snow. (By Rick Haithcox Photography.)

Sherman spoke for us both when he penned these words:

> *To alter a small part of the world and make it better is a worthy thing. To be part of a tapestry of noble works is to have lived in good times.*

Editor:
Beth Laney Smith

107

Chapter 9

Around the World in 76 Days

One of the pleasantest things in the world is going on a journey...

— William Hazlitt

Alene and I took a trip around the world in 1979 on the cruise ship the Rotterdam. We left in January and came back in April. Over the course of the trip, we visited: Florida, the Panama Canal, Aruba, Acapulco, Colombia, Los Angeles, Hawaii, Singapore, Thailand, Hong Kong, Japan, China, Russia, Istanbul, Egypt, Israel, India, Naples, Greece, Alexandria, Suez Canal, Lisbon, Ville France, and New York.

The whole vacation took 76 days. We left out of Fort Lauderdale with several members of the family joining us for this first leg of the trip: Catherine Stowe Pharr, Bill Pharr, Catherine Pharr Carstarphen, Catherine S.P. Carstarphen, Martin Carstarphen, Bill Pharr Carstarphen, Harding Stowe, and a family friend, Mary Sue Howe. Our first port of call was Aruba, Cartagena, South America, and then on through the Panama Canal to Acapulco. We continued to Los Angeles, where we spent a day at Disneyland, and then the rest of the family returned home.

One memorable stop along the way was Aruba, where the ship almost left without our young adults. Harding, Catherine, Bill and Martin disembarked and went to the beach to scuba dive, but they ran into some trouble getting back to the cruise ship. Luckily the young explorers returned just in the nick of time, as Harding recounts.

Dan and Alene boarding the Rotterdam cruise ship.

Dan was joined by several family members to depart from Fort Lauderdale, including sister, Catherine Stowe Pharr, and brother-in-law, Bill Pharr.

Dinner at sea was a black-tie affair. Pictured left to right: (front) Catherine Pharr, Mary Sue Howe, Catherine Ann Carstarphen, Catherine S. P. Carstarphen, Alene; (back) Martin Carstarphen, Bill Pharr, Dan, Harding Stowe, Bill Pharr Carstarphen.

Harding Stowe Remembers

Dan was planning his trip around the time I graduated from Clemson, and he invited me to come along. I mentioned the trip to my cousin Martin, because we are the same age, and by the time we left, the whole Pharr family was going.

It was an elegant ship with a very professional crew. It was much more formal than cruises are today. It reminded me of an older style cruise ship, because we had to wear a tuxedo to dinner every night while at sea!

In Aruba, Martin, Catherine, Bill, and I chose to explore the small island and go scuba diving. We took a cab without any trouble. But when our day at the beach was finished and we were ready to go back to the ship, none of the cab drivers would take us because our bathing suits were wet. We knew what time the ship was leaving, and they had told us that if we weren't on it, we'd be left behind. Finally, after an hour of trying

Dan's nephew, Harding, enjoying a swim, the sun, and plenty of skin!

The Rotterdam was equipped with several decks for lounging pool-side. Members of the family took advantage of the warm ocean weather: (back row) Catherine Stowe Pharr, sister; Dan Stowe; (front row) Bill Pharr, brother-in-law; Catherine S. P. Carstarphen, daughter of Catherine Pharr Carstarphen; Catherine Pharr Carstarphen, niece.

In Bangkok, Thailand, commuters traveled by boat through narrow canals. Much like the major thoroughfares of other cities, the waters would be jammed with boats trying to maneuver though small spaces.

Dan and Alene pictured on the deck of the Rotterdam. Alene remembers the elegant ship fondly, "You always had a home to come to at night after you've visited all those places. A cruise is the best way to travel."

to hail a cab, we found one driver that would take us back. When we pulled up, Dan was standing at the bottom of the gangplank along with a crewman who had his arms folded across his chest waiting to pull up the door. The gangplank was a great big door and when the crewman slammed it shut, you could hear it half a block away! Later Dan told us that just before we made it back, the captain said the ship could wait a few more minutes, but that was it.

It was a great trip for everybody. And I think from Dan's point of view, it was really one of the highlights of his extensive traveling experiences.

From Los Angeles, Alene and I made the trip by ourselves. We ventured into all the countries on the itinerary except for China, because it is a Communist country. Several people from the cruise took a trip inland, but Alene and I opted to stay aboard the Rotterdam. However, we were able to look out over China from a mountaintop in Hong Kong. We realized we had made a wise decision when most of the travelers returned and were very sick from the Chinese food and the meager accommodations.

Earlier in the trip, Alene and I grew weary of eating the cuisine in some of the countries. Neither of us wanted to spend any of the time we were traveling being sick. We vowed to drink bottled water at all the stops and eat sparingly. Before embarking on the trip, I had requested a small refrigerator for my cabin, and crew members kept it stocked with loaves of bread and jars of peanut butter. Every time we docked in a different country, and had planned a trip to see the sights, Alene would come over and pack peanut butter sandwiches in her large purse, bought specifically for the trip to hold such incidentals. They certainly came in handy!

On the Rotterdam, guests were welcome to host cocktail parties after dinner, where the cruise ship provided food and decorations, and the hosts provided beverages.

Many of the dwellings along the canals were three-sided, which allowed tourists and Thai residents to observe as children washed clothes, dishes, and bathed in the waters that serve as a main road through Bangkok.

While in Israel, Dan and Alene saw the site of the manger in which Christ was placed after his birth.

A highlight of the trip was visiting the Garden of Gethsemane, upon Mt. Olive. The olive trees are believed to have existed at the time Christ went to the garden before he was crucified.

Among several other sights, Dan and Alene visited the Blue Mosque in Istanbul.

Dan and Alene will never forget the big number 13 on their life jackets: "It looked like we were a lost cause—but we made it anyway!"

When we stopped in India, we were eager to see the Taj Mahal, and planned to join the tour group to see it. We got up at 2:30 in the morning to prepare to leave for the airport and fly into New Delhi. We visited the expansive Taj Mahal, which I had always wanted to see and was a high point of the trip. We returned to the airport, which consisted of a small cement room, ill-equipped with just a counter—no attendant. After waiting for an exceedingly long time, people began to worry. The tour guide kept saying, "Well, they say they're going to send a plane after us. We don't know when, though." Without a snack stand or vending machines, everyone started to get hungry. Not Alene and I! We sat in the corner, happily eating peanut butter sandwiches and "taking our medicine." Earlier in the trip, Alene had filled medicine bottles with drinks to accompany the peanut butter sandwiches — hers with Chivas Regal, mine with Jack Daniels! We laughed and enjoyed the long day — and night — spent in the wayward airport. We finally returned to the ship by 12:00 that night, just in time to eat the midnight meal!

The Rotterdam was a wonderful cruise ship, and offered many amenities. As Harding described, each night we were at sea, we dressed in formal attire for dinner. First we had cocktails, and then would adjourn to a black-tie dinner, followed by entertainment that sometimes suited the country we were visiting.

The cabin boy assigned to our staterooms, Ade, was very attentive and became a good friend to Alene and me. He would bring her milk to add to her bath, and even brought her flowers in Hawaii. At the time of the trip, Alene and I were not

Dan and Alene visited the Taj Mahal in India. It is set apart from the city, in a barren field outside New Delhi.

married, so we stayed in separate cabins. Ade was amazed, because most couples on the ships, married or not, stayed in the same room. He explained to us that in his homeland of Indonesia, your new bride must be a virgin on your wedding night, or her father had to take her back and give the groom back his wedding dowry! So I guess he was very pleased that we did not follow the more modern way of courtship.

Wherever the wind takes me I travel as a visitor.

— Horace

Dan and Alene visited Notre Dame, in Paris, France.

Our final stop was Ville France. We flew into Paris, where we visited for a couple of days before boarding the Concorde to fly to New York. We ate breakfast three times that morning: first in Paris, then breakfast on the plane, and then we ate breakfast again in New York. The plane was going so fast! At 60,000 feet high, the Concorde travels 1,400 miles an hour, so the entire ride took about three hours and 45 minutes.

It was a very enjoyable trip — just the excitement of being on the cruise ship, seeing all those places and being gone for so long. But really and truly, going all the way around the world made us realize when we came back home that there was nothing prettier than right here.

Editor:
Lauren Brisby

The ship stopped at some of the destinations for a few days, while stopping at some ports for only six to eight hours.

Chapter 10

Daniel Stowe Botanical Garden

The **1**dea That **K**ept on **G**rowing

"God Almighty first planted a garden; and, indeed, it is the purest of human pleasures."

—Francis Bacon

Native to the region: the Catawba Rhododendron. (Illustrated by John Steele, son of Bill Steele.)

There are few things I enjoy more than getting my hands dirty in God's good earth. My love of gardening came from my mother, who always kept the grounds at our North Main Street house in beautiful condition. She taught me the reward of watching a garden take shape under one's own hands. But as every avid horticulturist knows, gardening involves much more than simply planting seeds and digging around in the dirt. It is a way to explore nature, experiment with new ideas, and calm our minds—all while giving something back to the land. Gardening is, essentially, a way for *us* to grow.

Not long after I had accumulated Seven Oaks Farm, developers began to approach me with offers to build resorts or golf courses there. After some consideration I decided that I wanted to keep the land the way it was, for people to explore and enjoy. During childhood outings with my father, I had learned to identify types of trees and developed a deep respect for nature. The land is in my blood. The prospect of seeing it paved over for another country club saddened me.

(By Rick Haithcox Photography.)

Gazebos provide a restful place for visitors to gaze across the rolling landscape. (By Rick Haithcox Photography.)

The Budding of an Idea: A Conservatory on Seven Oaks Farm

Bill Steele: I met Dan during my employment at Wachovia, when I was assigned to his estate planning, and I had the pleasure of working with him in that regard for several years. Our biggest project, however, began after I retired. Dan knew of my retirement, and about six weeks after it took effect, he called and said, "Bill, could you fit lunch with me into your schedule?" Well, all I had to do that week was cut the grass, so there was no problem fitting it into my schedule!

I had lunch with Dan and Alene, and afterward we went into his study. In all the meetings we'd had in his house, this was the first time he closed the study doors. I thought, "This must be very serious."

Dan told me that he had seen in the **Charlotte Observer** an announcement of the opening of the Fuqua Conservatory at the Atlanta Botanical Garden. He said, "I think this may be what I want to do with my land." There's a knoll where Lower Armstrong Ford Road dead ends into South New Hope, and a beautiful old oak is growing at that spot. Dan pointed out: "You can see that oak from any approach. That area would be a prominent place to put a beautiful conservatory—but before I decide to do that, I want to learn more about what it would involve. Would you go to Atlanta, without telling anyone whom you're representing, and talk with them about the cost of building a conservatory?" I told him I would be glad to do this.

I went to Georgia and, through Boyce Lineberger Ainsley (my wife's cousin), was able to make a contact with the now late Ann Crammond, who at that time was the director of the Atlanta Botanical Garden. We discussed the costs of construction, plants, personnel, and heating and cooling.

I was not fully aware of this at the time, but Ann would become very important to the development of the garden. It would not exist if she had not been there with her warm, giving attitude. She could easily have brought the idea to a halt by saying: "Oh, it's so expensive. You wouldn't be interested in this. Your

So I wrestled with the matter of what to do with my land. Alene and I sought input from several family members and friends. Finally, in 1989, we came upon an idea that satisfied us: we would build a conservatory. This would not only preserve the Seven Oaks property, but would also optimize its beauty and encourage people to spend time with nature.

Although we both liked the idea of a conservatory, Alene and I did not automatically let that put an end to our consideration of other possibilities. The more we looked into what could be done with the land, the more potential we realized it had. Ten years later, what began as the plan for a single conservatory has ballooned into the colossal project that is currently a short distance from my house. Now, in place of the old cow pastures, thickets, and unruly tangles of undergrowth, is a full-size botanical garden. Alene and I have the gratification of knowing that 450 acres of land that I have made available will serve the community for many years to come.

(By Scott Gilbert.)

One man who is singularly qualified to talk about the history of the botanical garden is Bill Steele, former director of development. Bill became involved in the project shortly after I was inspired to build the conservatory, and he remained a vital participant in its planning and execution. He was the first executive director for the botanical garden, which meant it was his responsibility to supervise planning and construction. Bill served in that capacity until June 1996. He tells in his own words the story of how the garden came to be.

Ann Crammond, of the Atlanta Botanical Garden, provided insight and advice regarding the planning of Phase I. (By Steve Rankin Photography.)

visit other gardens. I'm aware that you and Harriette had planned to do some traveling, but if you could just give me a few hours a week until I can digest this thought process, I would appreciate it." I told him that would be fine. He then suggested:"Why don't you take Harriette with you? She would enjoy seeing the gardens."

So Harriette and I set off. We visited Longwood Gardens, outside of Philadelphia, and Lewis Ginter Botanical Garden, which is being built in Richmond. We also explored Chicago Botanic Garden, Missouri Botanical Gardens in St. Louis, New York Botanical Garden, Brooklyn Botanic Garden, and Callaway Gardens in Pine Mountain, Georgia.

During these visits, we met several people who would become very important in the development of the Daniel Stowe Botanical Garden (DSBG). Bob Hebb, director of the Lewis Ginter Botanical Garden, would prove to be

(By Rick Haithcox Photography.)

unnamed principle couldn't possibly afford it." And that would have been the end of it.

Instead, one of the most important things Ann told me was:"If your principal is sincerely interested in doing something of this caliber, he should not make a decision based on your interview with me. You need to talk to other people in this industry. I would be delighted to introduce you by phone to the directors of other gardens, and then you can set up appointments with them." She rattled off the names of about a half dozen botanical gardens that she thought I should visit.

Those names were included in a long memorandum I wrote to Dan. Ann also gave me quite a stack of information and printed material, and I took a number of photographs of the Fuqua Conservatory. I turned all of this over to Dan when I got back. And then I waited.

The Idea Takes Root: Research Excursions to Other Botanical Gardens

After he and Alene had reviewed the information and discussed it for a couple of weeks, Dan called and invited me to lunch again. At that meeting, he said:"Bill, I think we need to undertake this recommendation that you

The Robert Lee Stowe Visitor Pavilion. (By Amy Smith.)

Fountains and brick walkways are intertwined with blossoming flowers and greenery. (By Jim Leggett.)

enormously helpful. Since then, he has continued to guide and encourage us as we go forward. Dan's garden wouldn't exist if it weren't for Ann Crammond, first, and Bob Hebb, second.

Another person who has been indispensable is Fred Roberts, director of the Longwood Garden. He has been an incredible resource, and I've called on him again and again over the years. He has gone to the 99th degree for us countless times.

Harriette and I had already planned a trip to France, so we sort of changed gears and took in a number of gardens during our stay. We also laid over in England a few extra days, allowing us time to tour some of its botanical gardens—so we got a really good smear. I gathered notes and conducted interviews, and Harriette took photographs and videotapes of the sites. So this gave Dan and Alene some real insight into existing botanical gardens. After reports from each trip, their horizons were broadened, and their thoughts relative to his property were raised.

Hitting Pay Dirt and Digging In: The First Stage of Planning

Harriette and I made these trips for about nine months. After the last one, Dan said: "I think we know enough about it, Bill. Let's do an entire botanical garden, not just a single conservatory. What do we do next?"

The next step was to get someone to help plan the garden. In the meantime, I had joined the American Association of Botanical Gardens and Arboreta as an interested person—not as a professional. The association had a southeastern regional meeting at the Marie Selby Garden in Florida during the nine-month period when I was making all of those research trips. Ann Crammond suggested that I go too so that I could meet a lot of botanical people. I told her: "Mr. Stowe wants to keep this thing under wraps. He doesn't want people to know who he is or what I'm about." She replied,

(By Jim Leggett.)

Heads of the Garden Staff, past and present

Bill Steele: Director of development. Served as the executive director from the project's beginning until June 1996.

Mike Bush: Executive director since June 1996. Joined the staff in March 1993 as chief horticulturist.

Ed Ellis: Joined the staff as director of development, alongside Bill Steele, in spring 1999.

Jim Summey: Landscape superintendent.

D. Rae: Curator of the gardens.

Linda Lowry: Gift shop manager. Established the gift shop.

Bill Hilton, Jr.: Former director of education and research. Designed and led classes, seminars, and workshops. Served from 1997 through spring 1999.

In August, DSBG hosts an annual Balloon Glow. (By Jim Leggett.)

"I'll just introduce you as my protégé, so you won't have to deal with any questions about what you're doing"—which was very nice.

After some really helpful conversations with people from all over the Southeast, I collected recommendations for planning firms and came up with a list of 23 potential sources. Then I drafted a letter to these firms on behalf of my "unnamed principal who was interested in developing a botanical garden on a lake outside of Charlotte, North Carolina," and asked if they would be interested in creating the master plan. I got a range of material back—some very thoughtful work, and some that was obviously slapped together and tossed into the envelope.

Based on these submissions, I was able to eliminate 14 of the firms. Then Dan, Alene, and I reviewed the materials from the nine remaining ones. We invited the principals of each firm to come to Belmont so they could meet the Stowes and get a better feel for the project. They all arrived on the same day, and I took them on a tour of the site. Dan's farm manager, Mr. McCorkle, had been reared as a Wyoming cowboy, so he was a very capable horseback rider. He and Dan had honeycombed the woods with riding trails a while back. This made it possible for me to take the prospective designers all the way through the property so they could see it up close, rather than just standing at the edge of the woods and looking. Every one of them was elated with the indigenous plant life and the way the land moved.

Later, the Stowes and I narrowed the group down to three—a firm from Cambridge, Massachusetts; another from Walterboro, South Carolina; and one from Pittsburgh, Pennsylvania. By this time, Dan had assembled a group of friends and relatives to be on the Daniel Jonathan Stowe Conservancy, Inc., board of directors. So we had each of the firms make a presentation to the board. After the presentations, the board decided unanimously to go with Environmental Planning and Design, the firm from Pittsburgh.

Geoffrey Rausch was the firm's design partner for gardens, and he has worked with us continually since then. We've become good friends in the process, because we've sort of lived together off and on for almost a decade. He has been a wonderful man to work with. He is very creative yet has no artistic temperament. The people in his office are top quality, high caliber folks in every area.

The Dirt on the Daniel Stowe Botanical Garden

Location: 6500 S. New Hope Road, Belmont. The garden may be accessible by boat from Lake Wylie.

Acreage of Phase One: 110 acres

Anticipated cost of the entire garden: $150 million

Anticipated completion time for the entire garden: 40 years

(By Scott Gilbert.)

An aerial view of South Fork Farms
and what is now DSBG.

Focusing Our "Sites": Selecting the Garden's Location

Soon Geoff came to Belmont, bringing his team with him, and they started walking the property. They would come and spend an entire day walking—they'd vanish in the morning, and I wouldn't see them again until it was time to lock the gate and go home. And they came in all seasons. If it was raining, they put on their rain suits and were out there walking the site. If it was just so cold you couldn't stand it and the wind was blowing terribly, they were out there walking the site. And if it was a broiling, sunny day, they were out there walking the site.

After all this walking, they came back with proposals for the placement of the garden. They had prepared drawings for each potential location, illustrating the way they envi-

sioned a garden fitting into that particular space. Geoff would get out his posters and walk the entire board of directors through what would go here and there, and then we'd move to the next location.

The board voted for the site that was set away from the road, which we later found out was Geoff's favorite. About the time we made that decision, we learned that New Hope Road would be widened into four lanes during the next 15 years. This will jack up the traffic—particularly the big truck traffic. So keeping the garden off the road was a wise move.

We project that it will take about 40 years to build this garden. I'll be long gone by then, but I have already had a fantastic experience in the planning.

Daniel Jonathan Stowe Conservancy, Inc., Board of Directors

The Daniel Jonathan Stowe Conservancy was endowed by Dan and Alene Stowe in 1989 to establish and support the Garden. James B. "Jick" Garland, then mayor of Gastonia, formed the corporation and attained a tax-exempt status for the organization. The Conservancy's Board of Directors includes some of Dan's family members, longtime friends, and business associates. Dan is chairman of the board.

(By Rick Haithcox Photography.)

Founding Board of Directors:

Daniel J. Stowe, Chairman
John L. "Buck" Fraley, Vice-Chairman
James B. Garland, President
Robert L. Stowe III, Vice-President
William L. Steele III, Secretary/Treasurer
Alene Stowe
Catherine P. Carstarphen
Catherine S. Pharr
D. Harding Stowe
J. Robert Wren, Jr.
Richmond H. Stowe
Carolyn B. Branan
Elizabeth G. Wren
Rebecca B. Carter

Current Board of Directors

Daniel J. Stowe, Chairman of the Board
Alene N. Stowe, Vice-Chairman
James B. Garland, Vice-Chairman
Robert L. Stowe III, Vice-Chairman
D. Harding Stowe, President
Richmond H. Stowe, Vice-President
Elizabeth G. Wren, Secretary
J. Robert Wren, Jr., Treasurer
John M. Belk
H. Tate Bowers
Carolyn B. Branan
Catherine P. Carstarphen
Rebecca B. Carter
Johnathan L. Rhyne, Jr.
William L. Steele
William H. Williamson III
Director Emeritus: John L. Fraley, Sr.
As of August 2000.

Board of Visitors Members

Chairman: Bill Williamson III
Chancellor: James H. Woodward
Jane Avinger
James Babb, Jr.
Kat Belk
H.C. Bissell
Suzanne Crist Botts
David Cline
Bill Coley
John Corbett
Judy Crosland
Sharon Decker
Pepper Dowd
John Edgerton
Tom Efird
Glenn Eisenberg
John Fraley, Jr.
Martin B. Foil, Jr.
Parks Helms
George Higgins
Peggy Hynes

Edwin L. Jones, Jr.
Johnny Long
George Liles
Michael Marsicano
Pat McCrory
Alex McMillan
Caroline McMillan
Eric Mozer
Johan Newcombe
Pat Rodgers
Jocelyn Rose
Willie Royal
Janet Rudisill
Will B. Spence
John Stedman
William L. Steele III
Howard Virkler
Edward Weisiger, Jr.
Rex Welton
Joan Zimmerman

(By Scott Gilbert.)

Rhododendron catawbiense

You are cordially invited to

A GRAND CELEBRATION

announcing a new Botanical Garden

and the

Daniel Jonathan Stowe Conservancy, Inc.

4:30 until 7:30 O'clock   May 23, 1991

Seven Oaks Farm   Belmont, N.C.

Cocktails and Supper   Reply card enclosed

(Courtesy of Shirley Rankin.)

Sowing the Seed in Our Community

On Thursday, May 23, 1991, I woke up feeling like a seven-year-old child on Christmas morning. The day would be very special to me for two reasons: it was my 78th birthday, as well as the occasion of the garden's formal announcement. The Conservancy had put weeks of work into planning an elaborate three-hour announcement party. Invitations had been sent to 800 people, more than half of whom replied that they would be able to attend.

As the celebration drew near, truckloads of trees, bushes, flowers, and manicured grass were hauled in for planting near the interim visitor center. Unfortunately, the weather had ideas of its own. Several days of rain slowed the landscaping crew's progress, and their boss, Joe Carpenter, had to bring in workers from other projects to make sure the deadline was met. But gray skies could not dampen Bill Steele's optimism. He was overheard vowing to coworkers that the day of the celebration would be "86 degrees and clear."

(By Scott Gilbert.)

Honorable guests at the formal announcement party included governor and first lady of North Carolina, Mr. James and Dottie Martin.
(By Steve Rankin Photography.)

Loonis McGlohon provided musical entertainment at the party. (By Steve Rankin Photography.)

Make no little plans.
They have no magic
to stir men's blood.

—Architect Daniel Burnham

Some distinguished guests and board members honored Dan, one of which was the mayor of Gastonia, Jick Garland. (By Steve Rankin Photography.)

On the evening preceding the formal announcement, we hosted a neighborhood party at the garden site. A good number of local residents joined us, curious about what would be happening so close to their homes. We pitched lawn tents near the interim visitor center, and a caterer served lemonade, finger sandwiches, cookies, and other refreshments. Bob Hebb of the Lewis Ginter Botanical Garden was the guest speaker that night, and he did an excellent job of explaining what a botanical garden is, in layman's terms.

Thursday turned out to be a warm, beautiful day after all. Among the special guests at the formal announcement party were: **James Martin**, N.C. governor; **Dottie Martin**, N.C. first lady; **Estell Lee**, N.C. secretary of economic and community development; **Jim Polk**, N.C. director of minority affairs; **Johnathan Rhyne**, N.C. House minority leader; **Wayne Sterling**, director of the S.C. State Development Board; **James Ashworth**, mayor of McAdenville; **Jick Garland**, mayor of Gastonia; **Betty Jo Rhea**, mayor of Rock Hill; **Marshall Rauch**, former N.C. senator and chief executive officer of Rauch Industries; **Joe Carpenter**, chairman of Gaston County commissioners; **Joseph Brosnan**, president of Belmont Abbey College; **Bynum Carter**, president of A. B. Carter, Inc.; **Buck Fraley**, retired chairman of Carolina Freight; **Duke Kimbrell**, president of Parkdale Mills; **Bill Lee**, chairman of Duke Power Co.; **Wayne Shovelin**, president of Gaston Memorial Hospital.

(By Rick Haithcox Photography.)

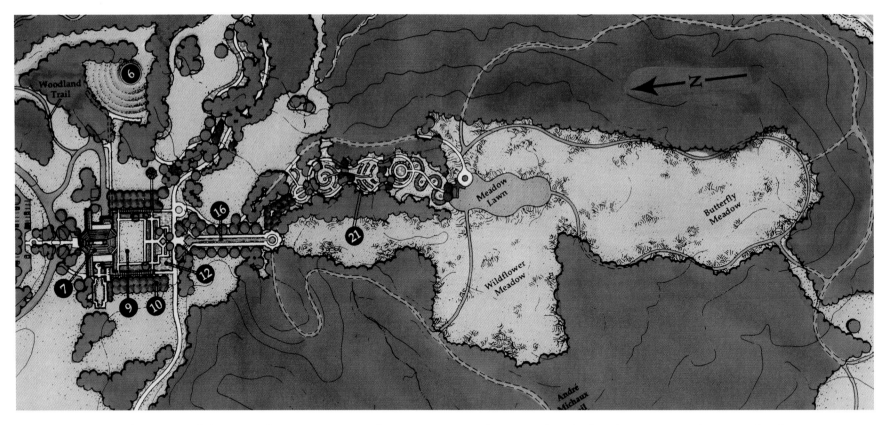

Phase One construction of DSBG: 6—Amphitheater, 7—Robert Lee Stowe Visitor Pavilion, 9—Four Seasons Garden, 10—Pergolas and Holly Walk, 12—Cottage Garden, 16—Canal Garden, 21—Perennial Garden.

The Garden Planners

Firm: *Environmental Planning & Design of Pittsburgh, PA*

Architect: *Geoffrey Rausch currently associated with: Marshall · Tyler · Rausch of Pittsburgh, PA*

(By Rick Haithcox Photography.)

Revealing the Master Plan

Budget constraints determined how much of the master plan could be executed during Phase One. Therefore Geoff Rausch's team and some of our representatives determined which components should be completed first. Initially, this phase was to include 106 acres, and that figure ultimately grew to 110 acres. This was a very exciting time—we were finally ready to begin construction of the permanent gardens. In June 1995, large trucks rolled in and workers began logging the site.

Phase One plans were officially unveiled on Thursday, August 10, 1995. A 27 foot willow oak had been placed in the ground for that ceremony, and I kicked off the new phase by shoveling a spadeful of dirt onto the tree. Children from local Daisy, Brownie, and Girl Scout troops helped finish planting it.

The interim garden remained open throughout the construction of Phase One, but toward the end of that period, workers gradually began phasing it out. Some of the perennials on display there were transplanted to the new gardens. The cottage and vegetable gardens located near the gift shop were among two of the beds that were maintained.

The grand Visitor Pavilion welcomes guests at the end of a meandering driveway. (By Steve Rankin Photography.)

Robert Lee Stowe Visitor Pavilion

The Visitor Pavilion is an expansive 13,500 square feet, crowned by copper roofing and a graceful spire over 50 feet high. You recognize the blending of architectural motifs, classical themes engagingly restated in a contemporary ambiance. The 20 white columns are of Tuscan design, simple in detailing and reassuring in strength. In quite a different mood is the dome surmounting Founders Hall, its Roman heritage enriched by stained glass of mesmerizing color.

Mike Bush discovered that mulit-colored dome at an eclectic antique shop, Great Gatsby's in Atlanta. The dome was crafted by talented designers, associates with renowned Tiffany. (By Rick Haithcox Photography.)

(By Scott Gilbert.)

Inside the Pavilion, guests can enjoy a scenic view of the gardens in the distance. The Great Hall leads directly onto the Four Seasons lawn. (By Steve Rankin Photography.)

The gift shop offers a wide array of garden products—from books, seeds and plants to gardening attire and nature-inspired jewelry. (By Steve Rankin Photography.)

(By Steve Rankin Photography.)

The dome allows a soft, yellow-tinted light to filter into the Great Hall. (By Jim Leggett.)

Proportions of the building are palatial, with lofty ceilings. But these classical details are not inhibiting. The architect has used great expanses of glass to remind you that this building is a companion to superb gardens.

The most commanding space of the building is the octagonally-shaped Great Hall, which extends beyond the foyer. It is aptly named, for its dimensions are 55-by-55 feet, with a ceiling that ascends to 45 feet. Walled with glass, the Great Hall provides an enticing view of the Four Seasons Garden and beckoning fountains beyond. The interior glass walls, which separate the room from the rest of the pavilion, may be draped with panels of fabric to create privacy for special gatherings.

Broad promenades on each side of the Great Hall give passage to the gardens ahead. They are also the display area for the black granite tablets engraved with names of the Garden's founding members.

Other spaces include a gift shop, meeting rooms for conferences and classes, the board room, and a serving area, which allows convenient catering for events. The facility also includes a full basement, encompassing an additional 13,500 square feet.

The grand Visitor Pavilion welcomes guests at the end of a meandering driveway. (By Steve Rankin Photography.)

Robert Lee Stowe Visitor Pavilion

The Visitor Pavilion is an expansive 13,500 square feet, crowned by copper roofing and a graceful spire over 50 feet high. You recognize the blending of architectural motifs, classical themes engagingly restated in a contemporary ambiance. The 20 white columns are of Tuscan design, simple in detailing and reassuring in strength. In quite a different mood is the dome surmounting Founders Hall, its Roman heritage enriched by stained glass of mesmerizing color.

Mike Bush discovered that mulit-colored dome at an eclectic antique shop, Great Gatsby's in Atlanta. The dome was crafted by talented designers, associates with renowned Tiffany. (By Rick Haithcox Photography.)

(By Scott Gilbert.)

Inside the Pavilion, guests can enjoy a scenic view of the gardens in the distance. The Great Hall leads directly onto the Four Seasons lawn. (By Steve Rankin Photography.)

The gift shop offers a wide array of garden products—from books, seeds and plants to gardening attire and nature-inspired jewelry. (By Steve Rankin Photography.)

(By Steve Rankin Photography.)

The dome allows a soft, yellow-tinted light to filter into the Great Hall. (By Jim Leggett.)

Proportions of the building are palatial, with lofty ceilings. But these classical details are not inhibiting. The architect has used great expanses of glass to remind you that this building is a companion to superb gardens.

The most commanding space of the building is the octagonally-shaped Great Hall, which extends beyond the foyer. It is aptly named, for its dimensions are 55-by-55 feet, with a ceiling that ascends to 45 feet. Walled with glass, the Great Hall provides an enticing view of the Four Seasons Garden and beckoning fountains beyond. The interior glass walls, which separate the room from the rest of the pavilion, may be draped with panels of fabric to create privacy for special gatherings.

Broad promenades on each side of the Great Hall give passage to the gardens ahead. They are also the display area for the black granite tablets engraved with names of the Garden's founding members.

Other spaces include a gift shop, meeting rooms for conferences and classes, the board room, and a serving area, which allows convenient catering for events. The facility also includes a full basement, encompassing an additional 13,500 square feet.

Performers included life-size butterflies and pianist Loonis McGlohon. (By Jim Leggett.)

Elegant banquet tables provided even more creative splendor for guests to admire. (By Jim Leggett.)

Finally it was time to execute our massive plan. The weekend kicked off with the arrival of The Princess. We welcomed her at the airport with champagne, flowers, and beaming board and committee members. The gala began at 7:00 in the evening on Friday, October 8, 1999. As the guests arrived, wearing formal attire, Her Highness greeted them, along with Harding and me, and other members of the Stowe family. We hired a limousine service to carry guests from Charlotte, Gastonia, and neighboring areas, some 260 in all. The partygoers entered through the expansive Visitor Center, where the focus was directed to a 12 foot flower arrangement. It was four-sided; one side to represent each of the four seasons.

As guests wandered through the garden, they were enchanted by purple, peach, and turquoise wings of butterflies, large enough to stand underneath. Guests sipped cocktails as they watched "statues" move ever so slightly, until their positions rendered something new. Sounds of a live harpsichord filtered through the garden. It was truly magical.

As many guests walked through the gardens for the first time, human statues added a unique element. (By Jim Leggett.)

Garden Cocktails

Pacific Duck Wonton Cups
Seared Tuna with Guacamole Drizzle & Mango Salsa
Parmesan Crostini with Prosciutto Di Parma & Chiffonade of Caesar
Fresh Goat Cheese Crostini with Sundried Tomato and Roasted Red Pepper Tapenade

Four Seasons Dinner
Under the tent on the Four Seasons Lawn
with dance music provided by the Loonis McGlohon Trio

Spring
Chilled Curry Asparagus Soup
Garnished with Coconut Crème Fraiche and Red Pepper Drizzle

Alois Lageder Pinot Grigio, Also Adige, 1998

Summer
Fresh Lobster Spring Roll with Ginger Caesar Tree
with Ginger Heirloom Tomato Salsa, Taro Chips and Tobiko

Chartron et Trebuchet Bourgogne Blanc, Burgundy, 1998

Fall
Grilled Filet of Beef Tenderloin, Roquefort Polenta Tower, Autumn Vegetables,
Cabernet Sauvignon-Balsamic Reduction

Château Croix de Rambeau, St. Emillion, 1996

Winter
A plate of miniature Frozen Sorbet Pears and Ice Cream Walnuts
with gold and silver dusted Chocolate Truffles

Prosecco, Nino Franco Rustica, Italy, NV

Featured Entertainment - Bobby Short

Dessert Finale
Enjoy the Visitors Center with music provided by Loonis McGlohon

Crêpes Cherries Royale   Petite French Pastries
Bananas Foster   Fruited Trifles
Dessert Cheeses with Fresh Fruits

(Courtesy of Pam Stowe.)

One of the most breathtaking visions at the party was the dining room within the tent. Giant banquet tables, each holding 30 people, were decorated lavishly representing the four seasons. Each table was a different season, and catered not only to visual beauty, but also to the sense of smell. For example, the Summer table was covered in yellow and gold sunflowers and the place settings were a mosaic created by summer vegetables. The Winter table basked in apples and cloves, pine cones and cinnamon sticks.

The extravagance continued with the Spring table, which included real working fountains surrounded by candles. The entire mid-section of the table was covered in fresh laid grass with blooming flowers.

All of the above photography by Jim Leggett.

Bobby Short, Featured Performer, came from the Carlyle Hotel in Upper East Side Manhattan to entertain guests. (Courtesy of Bobby Short Enterprises, Inc.)

We had sent 2,000 invitations, clad with real peacock feathers, and asked the price of $1,000 per couple. To ensure attendance, we decided to educate and share our excitement with the surrounding communities and friends prior to the party. Harding and I, plus other board members, spoke at several gatherings. For example, I went to Pam Kimbrell Warlick's book club meeting in Gastonia and several other friends of ours had dinner parties with 30 to 50 people in attendance, where we advertised the event. Ann Comer, one of the ladies from Pam's book club, relayed to me in a thank you note, "your enthusiasm for the event was contagious." This "pre-selling" technique was very effective.

Unless otherwise noted, all of the above photography by Jim Leggett.

ELIZABETH STETSON DOWD

Dear Pam,

Friday evening was the most beautiful gala Rodney and I have ever attended. You "out-did" yourself in making all the ingredients come together to provide guests with an exquisite palette which pleased all the senses.

The gardens themselves were spectacular and were enhanced by the gentle presence of mime sculptures and fluttering butterflies. The dinner tables, carrying out the four seasons theme, were enchanting with their magnificent flower arrangements. I have never seen such attention to detail.

The caterer did a splendid job and we always enjoy Loonis and his music. Bobby Short was "first class". His music took us on a pleasant trip down memory lane.

Your vision and sensitivity to the garden setting made the evening one we shall always remember. Thank you for assuming the responsibility of the gala and seeing it through with the flourish only you could have given it.

I am most grateful for the lovely Limoges box you gave me. It will be a wonderful reminder of the Stowe family, the gardens, and a fantastic evening.

Please extend my gratitude to Harding. He is a fine young man who is fortunate to have found such a capable and charming wife.

With admiration and affection,

Pepper

October 12, 1999

(Courtesy of Pam Stowe.)

(By Jim Leggett.)

As Bobby Short performed, and Princess Michael of Kent spoke of gardens around the world, the guests were charmed by our detailed planning and creativity. After the event, some of those attending wrote thank you notes to the garden and our family. I wanted people to go back and think, "You know, they really did it right." The gala made an impression and not only set a tone for the opening weekend, but for the success of garden events for years to come.

Pictured here at the event: (left to right) Christine Stowe, daughter of Robert Lee; Princess Michael of Kent; Lillian Stowe, daughter of Robert Lee; Palmer Stowe, daughter of Harding. (By Jim Leggett.)

(By Jim Leggett.)

(By Rick Haithcox Photography.)

The Ribbon Cutting

On Saturday about noon, the gates opened to the general public for the official ribbon cutting ceremony and Family Day. Past visitors were sure to notice one change immediately; the entranceway to the botanical garden was relocated several hundred feet from its original point on South New Hope Road, which allowed duck ponds and grassy foothills along the driveway. At the end of this route, guests witnessed for the first time the Robert Lee Stowe Visitor Pavilion.

Princess Michael of Kent attended the opening day festivities, and spoke of her own personal garden that contains 10,000 rose bushes, the largest rose garden in England, which she cares for along with only three gardeners. Like many of the visitors, Her Highness also planned to incorporate ideas presented at the garden in her own. She stated, "There are so many ideas here that I am stealing without any shame at all."

She also spoke of ideas displayed in her garden in England. Whereas a predominantly white garden may be common, she designed a "black and white" garden, including black tulips, pansies and irises. To the guests delight, The Princess told of a yellow, scented rose named in her honor, which luckily "resists black spot and mildew."

There were plenty of notable guests in attendance. Aside from Princess Michael of Kent, there was another member of royalty perusing the garden. Jerla Gross, better known as Queen Charlotte, made her first royal appearance at the opening. Queen Charlotte, who was in full attire including a hoop-skirt and parasol, greeted visitors and added to the charm of the southern landscape.

(By Scott Gilbert.)

(By Scott Gilbert.)

(By Steve Rankin Photography.)

The Reverend Oscar Burnett, of the Abbott of Belmont Abbey and the Chancellor of Belmont Abbey College, gave the invocation at the ceremony. He thanked God for allowing Dan Stowe the resources to create such an impressive display, with the tools of nature and beauty.

The guests clapped in anticipation of the latest developments to the garden, which they may now officially enjoy. The following family members and notables cut the flowery garland ribbon: Harding Stowe, Richmond Stowe, Robert Lee Stowe, Alene Stowe, Catherine Anne Carstarphen, Reverend Burnett, Bill Steele, Mike Bush, Geoffrey Rausch, B.D. Rodgers, Pat Rodgers, and Jick Garland. Alene hung the ribbon around her neck and smiled broadly as people flooded into the foyer.

Once the guests found their way to the garden and followed the herringbone path, they were entertained by such acts as Dale L. Brooks, the Magikal Minstrel, performers on unicycles, and children running under the spouting fountains. The proper names and species of all the plants were displayed on labels which encouraged guests to take note of varieties they may install in their gardens. On October 9, 1999, the much anticipated Phase I of the Daniel Stowe Botanical Garden was open for public exploration.

Surpassing Our Goals

In the beginning of the year, my good friend and executive director, Mike Bush determined a goal for the Membership Department to be accomplished by the year 2000. He encouraged the committee and staff to promote memberships with the goal in mind of reaching 5,000 members. This sounded like an improbable dream to most of the department. However, due in part to the holiday gift-giving season, we exceeded that aspiration. By December 31, 1999, we had enlisted 5,206 total members of the garden. By Spring, the names of all the contributors will be revealed on permanent plaques in the Visitor Pavilion.

(By Scott Gilbert.)

A Place for Botanical Display, Education, and Research

Education has been a primary focus from the start. The Interim Garden offered a variety of classes for children, as well as workshops for adults. The First Tuesday program, for example, was a series of monthly lectures presented by horticulturists from the Mecklenburg, Gaston, and York county extension services. These talks were free to the public, and the subjects addressed ranged from identifying rare and exotic species to planting one's own herb garden.

"I think that in its days of completion, Daniel Stowe Botanical Garden will have a major influence in educating the public on being more responsible with our land than my generation has been," Bill Steele once speculated. "All of the garden's classes have the same underlying theme: 'Let's be responsible stewards and preserve the green space for future generations.'"

(By Amy Smith.)

A Heart for Horticulture

Volunteers have been a vital part of DSBG from its beginning. Some have regularly assisted the garden's administration staff, while others have helped out periodically at plant sales and special events. Volunteers have also generously contributed countless hours of labor to the landscaping process.

In January 1999, the Hort Corps—a team of horticulture volunteers—was founded. The group works three days a week at digging, planting, weeding, mulching, raking, and pruning. The Hort Corps also assists in the garden's educational facet by photographing plants, and classifying and cataloging books for the horticulture library.

The Overall Picture

Due in part to growing tourist attraction to the gardens, the North Carolina Division of Tourism recognized Gaston as ranking 18th out of 100 counties, bringing in about $124 million in tourist revenue. The gardens are also considered an attraction to tourists visiting Charlotte and Mecklenburg County. The 35,000 visitors to the initial 10-acre sight of DSBG is expected to double following the unveiling of the new garden additions. In fact, Molly Gilbert, the marketing director for the gardens, projects the number of visitors could exceed 100,000 by the year 2000. Whereas in 1989, at the time Dan and Alene Stowe designated 450 acres of land and an adequate donation of money to begin developing Phase I, the garden was only 10 acres of development, it now spans across 100 acres.

Yet to Come

However, as far as Mike Bush is concerned, there is always room for building in the future. Currently plans are in the works for three additions: a restaurant, a waterway entrance, and an amphitheater. Many weddings are scheduled to take place in the gardens.

These additions may be open for public use within ten years; however, with the growing community support, could possibly be completed in less time. The restaurant is scheduled to be constructed next to the Visitor Pavilion, and serve as many as 300 guests.

Of the land on which the garden lies, some rests on Lake Wylie. In the future, boats may be able to cruise up to a waterway entrance and dock at the garden.

Finally, a 2,500 seat amphitheater will be erected to host musicians and other entertainment. At the 1999 Fourth of July celebration, guests lingered along the ponds and grassy hills to listen to the Charlotte Symphony. In the future, they will be able to relax in the expansive theater.

The Science Behind the Beauty

Less obvious, perhaps, is the role of research at DSBG, much of which has already been done (during Phase One construction) or will be done behind the scenes. As Bill Steele explains:

> *We started our research by doing analysis of the site's existing plants, flowers, trees, and shrubs, so that we can draw a line in the sand and see how it compares to what we have in the future.*
>
> *We are creating planted, tended gardens, and these are not always easy to maintain. Wind, birds, and bees move pollen and seed around, so that they escape from our tended gardens into the natural setting. We have to be alert to that and eradicate it, so that we are preserving what is supposed to be in the natural setting as well.*
>
> *We are also eradicating things that have migrated into that native, natural area, from previous inhabitation on the site. There are several plants that are not native to this area—certainly not in a woodsy setting—*

(By Rick Haithcox Photography.)

that have proliferated out there, because there's been nothing to impede them. We have to remove those and gradually, over time, take the woodland area back to what it ought to be.

Dan ran cattle on this property for 40 years, and they nibbled away a lot of the delicate plant material that was natural to the area. So we have already begun reintroducing the wildflowers and mosses and ferns that should be there and just don't exist.

In the process of doing this, we can also begin to do things in the future with plant culture. For example, we can take a piece of tissue from this native plant and put it in a petri dish and cultivate it so that it becomes a living entity. Longwood Gardens outside Philadelphia, while crossbreeding daylilies, has come up with some new varieties, and in crossbreeding roses [they have] come up with new varieties that they now market to the public as "the Longwood daylily" and "the Longwood rose." So this is something we can move into in the future quite inexpensively, without getting into a full scientific lab situation.

Editors:
Beth Laney Smith
Lauren Brisby

Birdsong and Butterflies

On a visit to the Garden on a hot afternoon in June, I discovered this new enchantment. We have come to expect a richness of blossoms and the graceful form of grasses. And of course we revel in the display and refreshment of the fountains. I sought to minimize the heat by resting in the shade of the East Garden House. And suddenly I am aware of the songs of many birds—such a variety that you'd think they were having auditions for a special performance. And they were all in good voice—trilling, warbling, showing off their best soprano notes. I have never heard such a bird concert before. And while I am still marveling, I left the Garden House and was visiting with the hollyhocks and other perennials. Suddenly there is a visitation of butterflies, of many species and colors. They settle on my arms and my shoulders and hover and dance around me. Birdsong and butterflies. I realize that within my experience I have discovered new hallmarks of the Daniel Stowe Botanical Garden.

—Beth Laney Smith

(By Scott Gilbert.)

(By Scott Gilbert.)

Index